PHILIP ALLAN
LITERATURE GUIDE
FOR A-LEVEL

TESS OF THE D'URBERVILLES
THOMAS HARDY

Mark Asquith

Series editor: Nicola Onyett

PHILIP ALLAN
UPDATES

Philip Allan Updates, an imprint of Hodder Education, an Hachette UK company, Market Place, Deddington, Oxfordshire OX15 0SE

Orders

Bookpoint Ltd, 130 Milton Park, Abingdon, Oxfordshire OX14 4SB
tel: 01235 827827
fax: 01235 400401
e-mail: education@bookpoint.co.uk
Lines are open 9.00 a.m.–5.00 p.m., Monday to Saturday, with a 24-hour message answering service. You can also order through the Philip Allan Updates website: www.philipallan.co.uk

ISBN 978-1-4441-1987-9

First printed 2010

Impression number 5 4 3 2 1

Year 2014 2013 2012 2011 2010

Printed in Spain

Hachette UK's policy is to use papers that are natural, renewable and recyclable products and made from wood grown in sustainable forests. The logging and manufacturing processes are expected to conform to the environmental regulations of the country of origin.

Cover photo: Justine Waddell as Tess in the 1986 film version of *Tess of the D'Urbervilles*. © ITV/Rex Features

Contents

Using this guide

Why read this guide?

The purposes of this A-level Literature Guide are to enable you to organise your thoughts and responses to the text, deepen your understanding of key features and aspects and help you to address the particular requirements of examination questions and coursework tasks in order to obtain the best possible grade. It will also prove useful to those of you writing a coursework piece on the text as it provides a number of summaries, lists, analyses and references to help with the content and construction of the assignment.

Note that teachers and examiners are seeking above all else evidence of an *informed personal response to the text*. A guide such as this can help you to understand the text and form your own opinions, and it can suggest areas to think about, but it cannot replace your own ideas and responses as an informed and autonomous reader.

Page references in this guide refer to the 2003 Penguin Classics edition of the text.

How to make the most of this guide

You may find it useful to read sections of this guide when you need them, rather than reading it from start to finish. For example, you may find it helpful to read the *Contexts* section before you start reading the text, or to read the *Chapter summaries and commentaries* section in conjunction with the text — whether to back up your first reading of it at school or college or to help you revise. The sections relating to the Assessment Objectives will be especially useful in the weeks leading up to the exam.

Key elements

Look at the **Context** boxes to find interesting facts that are relevant to the text.

Context

Be exam-ready

Broaden your thinking about the text by answering the questions in the **Pause for thought** boxes. These help you to consider your own opinions in order to develop your skills of criticism and analysis.

*Pause for **Thought*** ▐▐

Build critical skills

Taking it further boxes suggest poems, films, etc. that provide further background or illuminating parallels to the text.

Taking it **Further** ▶

Where to find out more

Use the **Task boxes** to develop your understanding of the text and test your knowledge of it. Answers for some of the tasks are given online, and do not forget to look online for further self-tests on the text.

Task

Test yourself

A cross reference to a **Top ten quotation** (see pages 90–93), where each quotation is accompanied by a commentary that shows why it is important.

❮ Top ten *quotation*

Know your text

Don't forget to go online: **www.philipallan.co.uk/literatureguidesonline** where you can find additional exam responses, a glossary of literary terms, interactive questions, podcasts and much more.

Synopsis

The novel charts through seven phases the brief life of a young milkmaid, Tess Durbeyfield, whose striking looks make her prey to the attentions of two very different men: the womanising cad, Alec D'Urberville, and the religiously inspired idealist, Angel Clare. In phase one Tess's father is told that he is related to the aristocratic D'Urberville family and gets so drunk that he is unable to drive to market. Tess goes instead but falls asleep and is responsible for the accident that kills the family horse. To make amends, a remorseful Tess agrees to visit a Mrs D'Urberville to ask for help. Unbeknown to them, the D'Urbervilles are simply successful business people who have recently moved into the area and have taken over the name. While there, Tess meets Mrs D'Urberville's son, Alec, who is immediately attracted to Tess's beauty. He encourages his mother to employ her and continually pursues her, eventually sleeping with her in the woods.

In the second phase, a pregnant and guilt-ridden Tess returns home, where her unsympathetic mother blames her for not forcing Alec to marry her. She returns to field work with her newborn baby and finds the villagers sympathetic to her plight. When the child falls sick and death seems inevitable, she is forced to carry out the christening herself. Following an angry exchange with the parish priest, she manages to get 'Sorrow' buried in the church grounds. Saddened by her plight, she decides to move elsewhere in search of a new start.

The third phase is characterised by the pastoral beauty of summer at Talbothays dairy. Here, under the benevolent guidance of dairyman Crick, she meets the young gentleman who rejected her at the Marlott dance, Angel Clare. He has rejected a university place, and the Christian orthodoxy of his family, in order to learn about farming. Tess and Angel fall in love but she is torn between a conscience that urges her to confess her past and her fear of losing him.

As, in the fourth phase, they move towards marriage, her continual attempts to confess (including a letter that goes astray) are thwarted. On their wedding night, prompted by Angel's revelations of his own romantic past, she tells him her secret — the narrative bringing the phase to an end.

The fifth phase begins with the end of her narrative and Angel's consequent rejection: she is not the woman he loved. After a few frosty days, he sails for Brazil, attracted by the farming prospects, and she returns home. Her parents remain unsympathetic and unscrupulously take advantage of her good nature to use the money Angel has given her to repair their roof. As a consequence, Tess is forced to look for work over the winter, finding it at Flintcomb-Ash. In harsh conditions that are the **antithesis** of Talbothays, she meets some of the milkmaids who have fallen on hard times. Encouraged by them, she eventually resolves to seek help from Angel's family, who are unaware of the marriage failure. Unfortunately, she overhears Angel's brothers and a former suitor, Mercy Chant, talking disparagingly about the marriage and she therefore runs away without meeting the parents. While walking back, she is shocked to see a newly converted Alec D'Urberville preaching in a cowshed.

In the sixth phase, The Convert, Alec pursues Tess all over again, claiming that he cannot sustain his faith in her company. He presents himself as reformed, offering to marry her and take care financially of her brothers and sisters. For some time Tess resists, but her mother's illness, her father's death, and the loss of the family home, lead to a crumbling of her determination.

In the seventh phase Angel returns from Brazil. His harsh experiences abroad and the words of a dying companion have convinced him that he has treated Tess badly. He tracks her down to a small seaside resort, Sandbourne, and, seeing that she is well provided for by Alec, leaves. Tess, distraught, accuses Alec of lying to her that Angel would never return and murders him in a fit of passion. She runs after Angel and together they evade their pursuers for a blissful week. Eventually, they are caught at Stonehenge, where Tess makes Angel promise that he will look after her younger sister, 'Liza-Lu. Tess is arrested and hanged.

antithesis contrast of ideas expressed by balancing words or phrases of opposite meaning, e.g. being cruel to be kind

Taking it **Further** ➤

Read Hardy's poem 'A Trampwoman's Tragedy' (1903) (available on www.victorianweb.org), which relates a true story that has parallels with the fate of Tess. Set in the vale of Blackmoor and written in strong Dorset dialect, it concerns the tragedy that arises from the love of two men for a single woman.

Chapter summaries and commentaries

PHASE THE FIRST *The Maiden*

Chapter I

*Task **1***

Read the opening two pages of Hardy's novels *The Woodlanders* and *The Mayor of Casterbridge*. How do these compare with *Tess of the D'Urbervilles*? Think about:
- Hardy's description of setting and character
- the syntax (word order) of the opening sentences
- the tone (focus on key words)
- how these openings prepare us for the story to come

Jack Durbeyfield is on his way home to Marlott when he is accosted by the antiquarian, Parson Tringham, who tells him of his descent from the 'ancient and knightly family of the D'Urbervilles', now extinct, and that he should reflect on 'how are the mighty fallen'. Ignoring such advice, the shiftless Jack immediately orders rum and a coach to carry him the rest of the way.

Commentary: **Through detailed references to actual geographical locations, Hardy creates a sense of verisimilitude — a feature emphasised by Durbeyfield's dialect. Hardy's decision to open the novel with this incident also foregrounds the theme of heredity that is to be central to the novel.**

Chapter II

The Blackmoor Vale is described in great detail and we are introduced to its historical legacy, particularly the killing of the white hart and the pagan fertility dance of the 'club-walking'. At this stage Tess is described as 'a mere vessel of emotion untinctured by experience', her momentary happiness destroyed by the entry of her drunken father. Three young gentlemen stop to observe the dancing and one, Angel, joins in. As he is leaving he sees Tess looking after him and wishes that he had danced with her.

Commentary: **Hardy introduces his main characters but, while Tess is associated with innocence, nature and fun, Angel is an outsider, a detached 'on-looker', his brothers snobbishly refusing to dance with country girls. His momentary indulgence sets up the irony that will dominate his relationship with Tess and he misses his chance to dance with her because he obeys the** church clock. Colour symbolism is important: Tess's white dress associates her with the purity and innocence of the hunted white hart, and through her red lips and the red ribbon in her hair Hardy launches a symbolic train through which he reinforces the inevitability of her tragedy.

Chapter III

Tess returns home and is told of her father's discovery, and her mother goes in search of John, who is out celebrating. When neither of them returns, Tess is forced to go to the Pure Drop in search of them.

Commentary: **We are introduced to the 'shiftless house of Durbeyfield', the 'unspeakable dreariness'. Hardy also indicates the personal qualities that will shape Tess's future: she has evolved beyond her family, which means that they are unable to understand her moral anguish later in the novel; furthermore, she feels a sense of responsibility for the family — 'a chill self-reproach' that she has been dancing while her mother has been working — which Alec will later manipulate.**

Chapter IV

At Rolliver's Inn Mrs Durbeyfield unfolds her plan to send Tess to 'claim kin', hoping that it may lead to 'some noble gentleman marrying her'. Tess and Abraham are forced to take hives to market early in the morning. Exhausted, Tess falls asleep with the result that the morning mail cart runs into them, killing their horse, Prince. Understanding its importance to the family, she blames herself, seeing 'herself in the light of a murderess'.

Commentary: **Joan's willingness to prostitute her daughter for economic gain is contrasted with Tess's readiness to take responsibility for the accident. It is this heightened sense of moral responsibility that will be her undoing. It is a chapter full of foreboding: Tess's pessimistic vision of the earth as a 'blighted one' seems vindicated by events. Her dreams of marriage to a handsome prince are ended by the spearing, as if by a lance, of her horse, Prince, which will in turn throw her into the arms of the false knight in shining armour — Alec. Hardy reinforces the fatalism through the red blood of Prince, which drenches her.**

Chapter V

Tess's guilt leads to her agreeing to visit Mrs D'Urberville. However, the D'Urbervilles are newly wealthy industrialists who have just adopted the

> **Context**
>
> Hardy questions Wordsworth's Romantic vision of 'Nature's holy plan'. These words are taken from Wordsworth's 'Lines Written in Early Spring' and reflect his belief that the beauty of Nature reflects the existence of a benevolent god.

melodrama

sensational dramatic piece with crude appeal to the emotions; also a staple Victorian literary and dramatic genre

Task 2

Write Tess's account of her first meeting with Alec. You should aim to write in Tess's voice, building upon Hardy's presentation of her character and capturing aspects of the writer's chosen form, structure and language.

name. At The Slopes she meets the arrogant Alec who, during a tour of the garden, makes clear his attraction.

Commentary: **Alec appears for the first time, the caricature womanising villain of melodrama with his moustache and 'bold rolling eye'. It is a meeting of experience and innocence, Hardy evoking the Garden of Eden, with Alec hidden behind his skeins of smoke, observing his Eve as she munches an apple. Colour imagery emphasises the sense of foreboding: Alec emerges from the 'dark' of the tent and adorns Tess's white dress with red. His forcing her to eat strawberries from his hand foreshadows his later seduction of her. Hardy amplifies the inevitability of events through the description of Alec as the '"tragic mischief" of her drama' and the 'blood-red ray in the spectrum of her young life'.**

Chapter VI

Tess receives a letter, purportedly from Mrs D'Urberville, offering her a job on the poultry farm. Despite misgivings, she gives in to family pressure and, spurred by her sense of guilt, agrees to go.

Commentary: **Hardy notes with great irony that the thorn of one of Alec's roses that pricks her chin is the only ill omen that she observed that day: as his careful use of colour has made clear, she is already ensnared in a tragic web. She had hoped to become a teacher, Hardy notes wistfully, but guilt for the death of Prince and compassion for her family's poverty drive her against her instincts back to Alec, a pattern that will be repeated later in the book.**

Chapter VII

Joan dresses Tess in the white dress she wore at the Marlott dance and takes her to be met by Alec. She is delighted when he appears in a gig and when Tess, despite some hesitation, sits beside him. Later that night she begins to wish she had made more enquiries about the man's character but quietens her doubts with the reflection 'if he don't marry her afore he will after'.

Commentary: **Hardy builds up the sense of foreboding by having Tess prepared like a sacrificial victim in a dress that emphasises her purity and innocence. Her misgivings are dramatised by her reluctance to mount beside Alec, which we observe at a distance through the eyes of Joan. It is her narrative perspective that allows Alec to become 'the handsome, horsey young buck' and it** is her reactions to events that are foregrounded to emphasise the extent of Tess's passive sacrifice.

Chapter VIII

Alec drives recklessly in order to frighten Tess into putting her arms around him. Eventually she is forced to allow him to kiss her and, though 'D'Urberville gave her the kiss of mastery', she quickly hatches her own strategy to get away from him. Having exchanged harsh words, they continue on their way, Alec in the gig and Tess walking.

Commentary: **Alec shows his true colours, his violent control of the horse offering a premonition of his treatment of Tess, who is merely a 'cottage girl' to be 'mastered'. Tess, however, proves feisty, not only in her openly wiping his kiss from her cheek but in her matronly observation that 'you ought to be ashamed of yourself…'. The chapter is laced with irony: Alec blames the character of his horse on fate, when the fate of another horse delivered Tess to him; and ironic foreboding in Alec's exclamation 'Kinsman be hanged!'**

Chapter IX

Tess is hired to look after blind Mrs D'Urberville's poultry, which includes whistling to them. Alec treats her with studied charm and civility, which 'removed most of her original shyness of him'.

Commentary: **Class is important: the removal of Tess to the deserted house identifies her as a servant and also foreshadows the family eviction later in the novel. She is also aligned with the caged birds, a common symbol in the Victorian period to indicate female vulnerability. Alec's whistling lessons are full of erotic overtones, not simply because of the sensual aspects of the pursed lips, but also because, according to Darwin, birds sing to attract a mate. Alec, therefore, releases her sexuality and covertly becomes her audience (see the section on 'Birds' on pp. 52–52 of this guide).**

Chapter X

Tess visits Chaseborough on Saturday night and when returning she refuses the offers of Alec, eventually parting with her work colleagues and getting caught up in an argument with an old favourite of Alec's, Car Darch, the Queen of Spades. Alec appears to ride to her rescue and Tess impulsively jumps up behind him — 'out of the frying-pan into the fire' as Darch observes.

Pause for *Thought*

How might the following feminist perspective enrich your reading of this scene?

'Alec's gig…is not simply the equivalent of a sports-car, his badge of machismo, wealth and social status. It is also a symbolic expression of the way in which Tess is deprived of control over her own body…whether by Alec himself or by the alien rhythms of the threshing machine.' (Mary Jacobus, *Women Writing and Writing about Women*, 1979).

Commentary: **The erotic atmosphere of the dance led to this event's excision from the Graphic version of the novel (and, therefore, from the 2003 Penguin Classics edition). The purity of Tess, who is 'on the momentary threshold of womanhood' is indicated by her refusal to go with Alec. However, she is undone by fate, it is her 'misfortune' to be caught laughing at 'the Queen of Spades', the latter's name reinforcing her symbolic function in the plot.**

Chapter XI

Alec takes a desperately tired Tess into the fog of The Chase — 'the oldest wood in England' — where he continues his wooing by announcing that he has bought gifts for her family. Deliberately losing his way, he stops to make a 'nest' for her while he pretends to go off in search of a landmark. Upon his return he finds her sleeping and, 'as the coarse appropriates the finer', he has sex with her.

Top ten *quotation* >

Pause for *Thought* ❙❙

Is Tess raped or seduced? Hardy is deliberately vague (not offending Victorian Morality), but references to the 'primaeval yews and oaks of The Chase' and Tess's ancestors suggest that to some degree Tess gives way to more primitive urges. What do you think?

Commentary: **The whole chapter, most of which was missing from the Graphic, is bathed in fog, which is entirely appropriate because we are not quite sure what happens. Hardy's outrage, however, is palpable, his awkward narrative intervention focusing on the purity of Tess while deriding the Christian idea of a 'guardian angel' or sense of justice. It happened because 'it was to be': fate is simply indifferent.**

PHASE THE SECOND *Maiden no More*

Chapter XII

Four months after her arrival at Trantridge, Tess eventually slips away. She maintains her dignity by refusing Alec's offer of compensation. He remains cynical about her suffering but also admits that he is a 'bad fellow'. She meets an itinerant sign-painter whose red slogans prick her conscience. When Tess arrives home her mother criticises her for not getting Alec to marry her.

Commentary: **Tess enters a relationship with Alec following her seduction, but then blames herself for her weakness. Her helplessness is articulated by her statement 'see how you've mastered me'. The sign-painter offers an attack on the cold rigidity of church morality, which foreshadows her later difficulties, and Tess instinctively exclaims: 'I don't believe any of it!' Experience has been the tutor of Tess, Hardy evoking the**

Eden motif in his assertion that 'she had learnt that the serpent hisses where the sweet birds sing...'.

Chapter XIII

Tess is momentarily uplifted by the envy of the other village girls, which demonstrates just how far her experience has elevated her above their innocent good humour. Depression soon sets in and she finds solace through the music of a church service and lonely walks at night.

Commentary: **Tess is driven from the church through idle gossip but she finds relief in music. Hardy's narrative in intervention emphasises that Tess is persecuted by her own overly sensitive moral guilt and that the 'voices antipathetic to her, was a sorry and mistaken creation of [her] fancy'. It is the upholders of rigid social laws that are out of harmony with the natural world, not Tess.**

Chapter XIV

The following summer Tess has had a child and is shown working with the harvesters, who treat her sympathetically. The child falls ill and, fearful for its soul, she calls for a priest to baptise him. Her father refuses to shame the family by letting the priest enter and Tess is forced to baptise the baby herself, naming him Sorrow. He dies and, having been refused burial on consecrated ground, is buried in an uncultivated portion of the churchyard.

Commentary: **The detailed description of the threshing adds to the sense of verisimilitude before, in a cinematic sweep, Hardy invites the reader to focus on Tess. Despite the camaraderie amongst the workers, this is no pastoral idyll: the red threshing machine is inexorable in its demands, punishing the women and making Tess bleed. Tess's experience has been her harvest and, when she is faced with the death of Sorrow, she becomes 'a being large, towering, and awful — a divine personage' in the eyes of her siblings. This is particularly apparent in her dealing with the village priest, whom she scorns for his lack of charity. It is left to the compassionate common sense of the village, particularly the sexton, to offer Christian, true, belief bound up in 'a little cross of two laths and a piece of string'.**

Pause for *Thought*

How might the following feminist reading enrich your reading of this scene?

Tess sees fit to 'repudiate a heaven that has no place for a newborn infant's unbaptised soul. Far from being a passive victim, Tess embodies a fierce impulse to self-determination against daunting, and ultimately insurmountable, odds' (Rosemarie Morgan, *Women and Sexuality in the Novels of Thomas Hardy*, 1988).

Chapter XV

For a year Tess works at home and becomes philosophical, musing on her beauty, her past experiences and her mortality. As spring comes

round she is offered work at Talbothays and, eager to start again, she resolves to go.

Commentary: **Experience and reflection transform Tess 'from simple girl to complex woman' who continues to dominate those who surround her. Her rejuvenation is linked to nature and the stirring of new life, the 'unexpended youth, surging up anew after its temporary check, and bringing with it hope, and the invincible instinct towards self-delight'.**

PHASE THE THIRD *The Rally*

Chapter XVI

Two and a half years after her return from The Slopes, the 20-year-old Tess is pictured on the road descending into the beautiful and fertile valley of Talbothays Dairy, singing in happiness as she walks.

Commentary: **Tess is an insignificant part of the landscape and yet she finds herself in tune with its vitality, hearing a 'pleasant voice in every breeze' which is part of the 'irresistible, universal, automatic tendency to find sweet pleasure somewhere, which pervades all life, from the meanest to the highest'.**

Chapter XVII

Tess joins the milking with the singing villagers and Dairyman Crick tells the story of how William Dewey used music to soothe an enraged bull. Tess recognises the gentleman who did not dance with her at the club-walking and that night in bed she learns that the stranger is Mr Angel Clare, a vicar's son who is learning about farming.

Commentary: **Talbothays is conjured up as a pastoral idyll, accentuated throughout by the symbolic use of sunlight and the prominence of the colour white in which singing milkmaids are governed by a humorous and benevolent Crick. Yet it remains real, a sense of verisimilitude being created through the use of dialect and the careful observation of details such as the bodily posture during milking. Angel is reintroduced, but he is not the impulsive student who danced with the girls. Rather he has seemingly lost direction in life and he is 'more thoughtful', with the air of something 'educated, reserved, subtle, sad, differing' about him.**

Chapter XVIII

Hardy begins by telling us how the 26-year-old Angel came to be at the farm. Because he is unable to accept the dogma of his father's **Evangelicalism** he is not sent to university like his brothers but instead spends time in 'desultory studies' and is nearly 'entrapped by a woman much older than himself' before eventually trying farming. At breakfast one morning he notices Tess, and inwardly remarking on her beauty he begins to take an interest in her.

Commentary: **Before Hardy allows his lovers to meet he introduces us to those aspects of Angel's history that are to have a bearing on their relationship. His defiance of his father and resulting 'indifference to social forms' displays the character that will enable him to marry Tess, but also the stubbornness that will cause him to reject her. His newfound intellectual humanism leads him to idealise the country life and particularly Tess as a 'genuine daughter of Nature' — a vision that is to have terrible consequences. Such ominous details are amplified by symbols of foreboding, such as Dairyman Crick's knife and fork taking the shape of 'the beginning of a gallows'.**

Chapter XIX

During a garden walk after work Tess is captivated by the sound of Angel's harp. The stilted conversation that follows focuses on their mutual melancholy.

Commentary: **Despite this unconscious appeal, Tess consciously admires Angel as an 'intelligence'. Their conversation underlines their mutual pessimism and also the poverty of words in articulating the feelings of lovers — a common Hardy theme. As the chapter closes Tess asks Dairyman Crick whether Angel might not be impressed by her lineage, but she is told to keep it quiet because of his disdain for hereditary privilege — a pose that is entirely in accordance with Angel's tendency to transform the world into generalisations.**

Chapter XX

Summer develops and their love grows as they are thrown together in the early mornings.

Commentary: **Talbothays is presented as a pastoral idyll or Arcadia, its misty mornings allowing Angel to idealise Tess as 'a visionary essence of woman' and his Artemis (the Greek goddess**

Evangelicalism

Protestant movement popular among the working classes in the nineteenth century. It emphasised the absolute truth of the Bible, the centrality of the Fall and original sin, and redemption through faith alone rather than good works.

❮ Top ten *quotation*

of chastity) before the sun (which shone on her in her youth) rises to reveal her in the flesh. She remains more cautious, appealing to him to 'call me Tess'. Hardy is insistent on the operation of fate, emphasised by the description of a 'clockwork' universe in the opening description of the seasons, the flight of the herons, and the inevitability of their relationship, which sees them 'converging, under an irresistible law, as surely as two streams in one vale'.

Chapter XXI

According to folklore, the failure of the butter to form leads to speculation that somebody is in love. Dairyman Crick relates the humorous story of Jack Dollop, who is himself churned in a milk vat by an angry mother until he agrees to marry the daughter he has wronged. Tess is upset by the parallels with her own story and leaves, after which the butter immediately forms. At night she overhears the other milkmaids whispering of their love for Angel, but Marian points out his attraction to Tess. Tess begins to entertain thoughts of love, but resolves that she 'could never conscientiously allow any man to marry her now'.

Commentary: **The tale of Jack Dollop serves to highlight Tess's over-sensitivity to her own moral plight. This trait is emphasised further by her reaction to the whisperings of the other milkmaids: despite their mutual attraction she remains determined to act according to her own strict moral code.**

Chapter XXII

The butter has a tang of garlic and, as everybody searches for the shoots, Tess attempts to draw Angel's attention to the other milkmaids while resolving to avoid him.

Commentary: **A chapter in which Hardy underscores his evocation of the pastoral idyll with a vein of realism. We see the consumptive 'Frances' lined up with the idealised Tess. Hardy's sharp description of the scene is designed to add to the sense of verisimilitude in the novel, while the hidden garlic plant that infects the whole symbolises the secret of Tess. Hardy uses the selfless behaviour of Tess to emphasise her purity once again.**

Chapter XXIII

The milkmaids find the road to church flooded and Angel carries them over one by one, admitting to Tess that he had left the pleasure of carrying her until last. The others recognise his preference and bear her no malice, but later in their dormitory they inform her that his parents have already chosen a wife of similar class for him.

Angel (Peter Firth) carrying Tess (Nastassja Kinski) in Polanski's film version of 1979

Commentary: **A strangely erotic scene (so much so that the Graphic version had Angel transporting the girls by means of a wheelbarrow!). Despite their proximity, Angel refuses the opportunity to kiss Tess, which contrasts not only with the passionate Alec but also with the milkmaids themselves, who are described as oppressed by 'an emotion thrust on them by cruel Nature's law'.**

Chapter XXIV

As Angel milks he can restrain himself no longer and, stealing upon Tess, he takes her in an embrace and declares his love for her. Tess cries and tries to withdraw.

Commentary: **Angel's desire is contextualised within an eroticised nature with its 'heavy scents' and 'oozing fatness and warm ferments...when the rush of juices could almost be heard below the hiss of fertilization', where he finds himself studying the 'curves of those lips'. Symbolically it is significant that Angel should declare himself when the sun is at its highest, which contrasts with the darkness of Alec's seduction. There is hope in the fact that he is attracted to Tess because of her physical flaws, but this turns into bitter irony when he rejects her for her moral imperfections.**

Pause for *Thought*

Hardy concludes this phase of Tess's life with a declaration that 'since Crick's last view of them something had occurred which changed the pivot of the universe for their two natures'. What is it?

Renn/Burrill/SFP/The Kobal Collection

PHASE THE FOURTH *The Consequence*

Chapter XXV

Angel reflects on his new-found passion and resolves to seek advice from his parents. On his way to Emminster he meets Mercy Chant, the preferred choice of his parents. After the natural country life of Talbothays he now feels like an outsider in the family home, which is stifling in its talk of religious doctrines.

Commentary: **Hardy opens the chapter with an analysis of Angel's mental state, its apparent awkwardness resulting from the fact that we are actually privy to his thought processes. Thus, despite his acknowledgement that 'he was driven towards her by every heave of his pulse', he finds himself virtuously but clumsily conceding that it would be wrong to trifle with her because her life was the 'single opportunity...vouchsafed to Tess by an unsympathetic First Cause'. Angel remains theoretical even in his passion. Hardy's depiction of Emminster gives him an opportunity to attack various strands of the church: Mercy is starched and prim; his father is 'an Evangelical of the Evangelicals' whose dogma is without 'aesthetic, sensuous, pagan pleasure'; and his brothers are 'unimpeachable models as are turned out yearly by the lathe of a systematic tuition' — narrow-minded pedants wrapped up in doctrinal debate.**

Angel remains theoretical even in his passion

Chapter XXVI

Angel talks to his parents about Tess and, while not rejecting his choice (provided she is orthodox in her faith), they praise the virtues of Mercy. His father tells him of the insults suffered at the hands of 'a young upstart squire named D'Urberville'. Nevertheless he remains hopeful that 'those poor words of mine may spring up in his heart as a good seed some day'.

Commentary: **The chapter is laced with irony: Angel perceives his parents' Christianity as something to be indulged and therefore paints Tess as an 'unimpeachable Christian'. Yet his description of her as 'brim full of poetry — actualized poetry' combined with his insistence that she is as 'virtuous as a vestal' (virgin) reflects his own narrow-minded idealisation. The mention of Alec prepares for his re-entry in The Convert, something that Hardy emphasises through his reference to the symbol of the D'Urberville coach.**

Task 3

Write this meeting from the perspective of either Angel's mother or father.

Chapter XXVII

Angel returns to Talbothays and asks Tess to marry him. Tess acknowledges her love for him but refuses, citing their difference in class. Angel rejects her excuse but changes the subject to his father's encounter with Alec. Tess, feeling her past creeping up on her, resolves not to accept him.

Commentary: **The contrast between the vicarage and Talbothays is accentuated by the description of Angel 'throwing off splints and bandages' and the erotic description of Tess as she wakes from a nap. Hardy views her from Angel's perspective, dwelling on her naked arm and neck, but also the mouth, hair and drooping eyelids that transform her into the snake in the Garden of Eden. Hardy reinforces the Eden motif by his description of Tess regarding Angel 'as Eve at her second waking might have regarded Adam' — the emphasis falling on the second.**

...drooping eyelids that transform [Tess] into the snake in the Garden of Eden

Chapter XXVIII

The chapter focuses on the struggle of Tess's conscience to resist Angel's pressure to marry. In an agony of indecision she agrees to give her reasons on Sunday, but finds herself drifting towards acceptance.

Commentary: **Hardy employs pathetic fallacy to dramatise the struggle between her desire and her scruples in the form of the thicket of pollard willows 'tortured out of their natural shape' in which she hides to avoid Angel's questioning. The pressure on her is described as physical; she is a 'sheaf of susceptibilities' and 'every wave of her blood, every pulse singing in her ears, was a voice that joined with nature in revolt against her scrupulousness'. She eventually finds herself giving in 'to snatch ripe pleasure before the iron teeth of pain could...shut upon her'.**

Chapter XXIX

On Sunday, Dairyman Crick tells the latest adventures of Jack Dollop, who has been deceived into marriage by a woman who did not tell him the full facts of the case. This leads to a general questioning of what a potential bride should tell. Angel continues to pressure a crumbling Tess who 'knew that she must break down'. After a final refusal, she agrees to drive milk to the station with him.

Commentary: **Crick's stories cast the struggle of Tess into a humorous light, and they also remind us of the pragmatic attitudes of the other dairymaids, summed up by Beck Knibbs's**

observation 'All's fair in love and war.' Angel's wooing has also altered to show uncomfortable parallels with Alec's chauvinism. He has resolved a new 'plan of procedure' founded on a 'more coaxing game' — which involves 'playful' accusations that she is a flirt. Tess's trust in him, however, remains undaunted, Hardy ironically noting that she regarded him as a man 'who would love and cherish and defend her, under any conditions, changes, charges, or revelations'.

Chapter XXX

In the dusk and rain Angel and Tess drive to the station. Tess attempts to reveal her past but is continually interrupted by Angel's patronising observations, and eventually she gives up and agrees to marry him.

Commentary: **The sunny pastoral innocence of Talbothays has been replaced by darkness, the grim realities of rural economics, and the intrusive, hissing machinery of the steam train. The journey also has obvious parallels with the first ride with Alec (Angel feeds Tess blackberries, Alec strawberries), but Angel's steadiness contrasts with Alec's wild gallop. Why doesn't she tell? First, because Angel doesn't let her: he continually patronises her, claiming 'you are a child to me' who could not possibly have felt trouble. Second, because she gives in to the 'appetite for joy' that pervades all creation. When she eventually accepts, Hardy describes how Angel learns 'what an impassioned woman's kisses were like upon the lips of one whom she loved with all her heart and soul' — which makes a mockery of his claims to her innocence.**

Chapter XXXI

It is now October and Joan Durbeyfield writes advising Tess not to 'say a word about your Bygone Trouble to him'. Angel presses Tess to name the date and announces their engagement. The generosity of spirit displayed by the other dairymaids makes Tess resolve to tell Angel everything.

Commentary: **Like the tales of Jack Dollop, Joan's advice may be self-interested and lacking in scruples but it is perhaps more in keeping with the harshness of the rural world. Significantly, Tess receives the advice as a means of shifting responsibility from her own shoulders, which leads to an intensification of her love. The love affair that blossomed in the early morning sun of Talbothays is now conducted in the afternoon sun of October, and although Tess walks 'in brightness' there are 'shapes of darkness' and**

Taking it *Further*

Compare the novel version with the scene from the 1998 television film with Justine Waddell playing Tess. How far does this interpretation fit in with your own thoughts about the text?
www.youtube.com/watch?v=HmaK0yBoBBU

shadows closing in on them. Hardy's examination of their emotions gives the reader ample grounds for concern: Tess's worship of Clare as 'the perfection of masculine beauty, his soul the soul of a saint, his intellect that of a seer' is grating in its immaturity, while the description of Angel's fastidious emotional life, in which he elevates the 'imaginative and ethereal' over the actual, warns us of his unhealthy capacity for idealisation.

Chapter XXXII

It is November and Tess still has not set a date. However, the need to reduce milking capacity leads Crick to suggest to Angel that when he leaves in December he take Tess with him as his wife. Tess reluctantly fixes the day for 31 December. Angel resolves to study the workings of the flour mill at Wellbridge, which also affords the opportunity to enjoy a honeymoon in an old D'Urberville manor house.

Commentary: **Hardy engineers events to conspire against the best intentions of his heroine, projecting her towards the marriage she so desperately wants but feels morally bound to resist. Angel's opting for a marriage licence (which removes the possibility of the marriage being questioned in church) leads to the wry authorial observation 'how events were favouring her!' And yet despite her growing sense of 'fatalism' she remains uneasy, worrying that 'all this good fortune may be scourged out o' me afterwards by a lot of ill'. There are enough omens to vindicate her foreboding, not least the honeymoon venue and the wedding dress that reminds her of the ballad of the mystic robe — a dress that changes colour if the wife has been unfaithful.**

Chapter XXXIII

While in town, Tess is insulted by a stranger, whom Angel impetuously knocks down. Worried by the event, Tess resolves to deliver a letter of confession, which she pushes under his door. Unfortunately, the letter goes astray. After one last attempt to confess, she marries in a state of 'ecstatic solemnity'. The bad omens, however, continue.

Commentary: **The incident with the Trantridge man demonstrates both the difficulty Tess has in escaping her past and also Angel's blind determination to believe only good of his future wife. Hardy has been much criticised for the device of the letter going astray, but it raises suspense and reinforces the sense of Tess battling against forces beyond her control: the ingredients of tragedy. The sense of impending catastrophe is highlighted by**

Hardy's meditations on the nature of their love. Whereas the emotionally limited Clare 'did not know at that time the full depth of her devotion', she perceptively observes 'she you love is not my real self, but one in my image; the one I might have been'. The sense of foreboding is increased by the introduction of omens such as the D'Urberville coach and the cock crowing — a biblical symbol of betrayal.

Chapter XXXIV

Wellbridge is a depressing place, made more so by the ominous portraits of the D'Urberville women. Angel dresses Tess in family jewellery, but confesses that he prefers the country girl. A message arrives announcing that Retty has tried to drown herself and Marian has been found 'dead drunk'. Tess resolves to confess, particularly following Angel's story, which mirrors her experience.

The legacy of Tess's hereditary disposition is depicted in the features of her ancestors

Commentary: **The legacy of Tess's hereditary disposition is depicted in the features of her ancestors, which are 'suggestive of merciless treachery'. Angel notes the similarity, but seems oblivious to the implications as he dresses Tess to look like them. Angel's confession emphasises the double standards of society: his tone is light, almost jocular, and he never doubts forgiveness. Despite Tess's generous forgiveness and palpable relief, Hardy guides us to find her subsequent confidence in reciprocal generosity misplaced. Her confession is given amidst the 'red-coaled glow' of the fire while the 'large shadow of her shape rose upon the wall'. She takes on serpent qualities as her eyelids droop down and the jewels transform her into a witch with a 'sinister wink like a toad's'.**

PHASE THE FIFTH *The Woman Pays*

Chapter XXXV

Angel is stunned by her story and, unable to come to terms with the new Tess, he walks in the fields, Tess following meekly, drawing attention to his hypocrisy. Upon their return his heart is hardened further by the sight of the D'Urberville portraits.

Commentary: **Nothing has changed but the entire texture of their surroundings has been altered by her words. Angel is cruelly undemonstrative, at one stage waiting 'patiently, apathetically,** till the violence of her grief had worn itself out'. Shocked out of his idealisation, his announcement that 'the woman I have been loving is not you' is both true and indicative of his lack of emotional depth. Unable to face his own limitations he turns on Tess, accusing her of duplicity in her 'present mood of self-sacrifice and your past mood of self-preservation' and betraying an ingrained snobbery in his labelling of her as 'an unapprehending peasant woman'. Only momentarily does he question his reaction, but this is dismissed when he catches sight of the framed pictures. Tess fires up with some righteous indignation but generally she is crushed, following Angel with 'dumb and vacant fidelity' like a 'wretched slave'.

Chapter XXXVI

For three days the couple maintain a studied normality. When Tess suggests that she return to her family, Angel agrees.

Commentary: **The chapter reveals the stubbornness of Angel's character, 'a hard logical deposit, like a vein of metal in a soft loam' that makes him inflexible. His lack of emotional depth makes him contemptuous of emotions in others. He remains a humanist lacking the depth of human emotions. Tess remains pure. Hardy notes that she 'might have' used her physical charms to win him round but refuses to lower herself. Instead, such is her self-loathing that 'she took everything as her deserts'.**

❮ Top ten *quotation*

Chapter XXXVII

Angel sleepwalks and carries Tess to an open tomb in the ruined abbey, where he lays her. The next day he is unaware of his actions and both set out for a visit to Talbothays. They agree to part, Angel forbidding her to contact him by any means but letter.

Commentary: **This scene dramatises Tess's trust in Angel and also his repressed feelings. Significantly, Tess understands that the revelation of this truth would do more damage than good, reasoning that 'he had instinctively manifested a fondness for her of which his common-sense did not approve; that his inclination had compromised his dignity when reason slept'. Upon their return to Talbothays the soured relationship is depicted through pathetic fallacy as 'the gold of the summer picture was now gray, the colours mean, the rich soil mud, and the river cold'.**

Context

A melodramatic scene in which Hardy strays into the genre of the Gothic, playing upon the Victorian fascination with Mesmerism (a precursor of hypnotism), which was believed to be a means of revealing the subconscious, or 'repressed' feelings.

Chapter XXXVIII

Tess returns home, but is so shocked by her parents' reception that, after giving them half the money donated to her by Angel, she leaves.

Commentary: **Tess's scrupulous morality has no place in the Durbeyfield home, a fact indicated by her inability to get into her old room. Her mother berates her as a simpleton, her father doubts the validity of the marriage, yet Tess refuses to slander Angel. Her decision to donate money to her parents emphasises her idealistic goodness. It also exposes her to the financial pressure exerted by Alec later in the novel.**

Chapter XXXIX

Three weeks after their separation Angel goes back to Emminster. He also conceals the true situation from his parents and endures his mother's good-intentioned praise of Tess, but while defending her purity, he is unable to forgive her for what he perceives to be her duplicity.

Commentary: **The Clares are liberal but are able to conceive of Tess only in relation to biblical references, a blinkered perspective as dangerous as Angel's pastoral idealism. Angel dismisses them as simpletons, but is himself censured by Hardy as 'the slave to custom and conventionality' living in 'the shade of his own limitations'. He also articulates an argument that becomes central to his defence of Tess's purity throughout the rest of the novel: that 'moral value' should be measured not by acts but by intentions.**

Task 5

Try to locate two or three examples during the visit when the attitude of Angel's parents is being used in an ironic way.

Chapter XL

Angel attempts to shock Mercy Chant by whispering anti-religious sentiments to her. He later meets Izz Huett and offers to take her to Brazil with him. She agrees but, when she admits that nobody could love him as much as Tess, Angel is brought to his senses and is 'within a feather-weight's turn' of joining Tess. He remains, however, inflexible.

Commentary: **Hardy emphasises Angel's mental breakdown in this chapter. Like Tess he is presented with two people who appeal to different aspects of his character, but his cruelty to both is a contrast: it is a chapter in which 'women pay'. Izz proves herself as honest as Tess and pays the price of what he passes off as 'momentary levity'. His only redeeming feature is that he is moved by the love of Tess but this is soon crushed by the logical conclusion that 'if he was right at first, he was right now'.**

Chapter XLI

Eight months have passed and the money left by Angel has all but disappeared, a large portion going on a new thatch for her parents' cottage. Too proud to ask the Clares for money, Tess sets out to join Marian on an upland farm. Accosted on the road by the Trantridge man Angel had knocked down for insulting her, she hides in a plantation surrounded by dying pheasants.

Commentary: **This emphasises the vulnerability of all living things in Hardy's harsh universe. We learn in an authorial aside that the English farmers who had made the journey to Brazil were now suffering the harshness of the Brazilian climate. Tess suffers unwanted male attentions and is transformed into a hunted bird forced to build a nest for herself among the wounded pheasants. The birds are 'kindred sufferers' at the hands of men who 'made it their purpose to destroy life'. It also allows Hardy to demonstrate Tess's compassion, as she immediately forgets her problems to attend to their suffering — as 'she killed the birds tenderly'.**

Chapter XLII

Tess trudges on, protecting herself from future male interference by disfiguring herself. Arriving at Flintcomb-Ash, Marian is shocked at her appearance. Tess writes to her parents but refuses to tell them of the harshness of the conditions, to protect Angel from their reproach.

Commentary: **Flintcomb-Ash is the destiny to which Tess 'was doomed to come' and through a process of pathetic fallacy it offers a picture of her internal distress that contrasts with the happiness of Talbothays: it is winter rather than summer; the farm is harsh and inhospitable — 'sublime in its dreariness'. The farm also offers an insight into the harshness of rural conditions, the punishing work presided over by the chauvinistic bully, farmer Groby, who offers a contrast to the affable Dairyman Crick.**

Task 6

Note down some quotations that indicate the harshness of the environment. (Think about the work they are doing and the contrasting parallels with Talbothays.)

Chapter XLIII

Tess and Marian endure the hardships of field work, the former by dreaming, the latter by drinking. They talk of old times and Tess learns of Angel's proposal to Izz. She resolves to write to him, but is unable to finish the letter.

Commentary: **Hardy clearly admires the stoicism of the female workers and stylistically offers a realist depiction. The natural rhythms of Talbothays have given way to economic necessity: 'Marian said that they need not work any more. But if they did not work they would not be paid; so they worked on.' Birds are important in the chapter, both the herons, whose indifference to all the disasters they observe offers an object lesson in survival, and the image of Tess as a 'bird caught in a springe'. Essentially the harshness of the conditions, the severity of Groby and the Amazonians, and the news of Angel's betrayal are designed to test the resolution of Tess.**

Chapter XLIV

Worried at having not heard from Angel, Tess decides to visit his parents in Emminster. The Clares are not at home and she hears Cuthbert, Felix and Mercy Chant discussing Angel's unfortunate decision to '[throw] himself away upon a dairymaid'. Tess trudges away. On the road she pauses to listen to a fiery preacher and is shocked to find that it is Alec.

Commentary: **It is another journey of dashed hopes. She sets off in the middle of a winter's night to 'win the heart of her mother-in-law' but is easily dissuaded from carrying her plan through. Hardy indicates a fatal lack of confidence: she even claims that the church tower in which Clare is delivering his sermon looks 'severe'. Fate is also dominant: she narrowly avoids meeting the wrong Clares, who, in a highly stylised piece of drama, articulate her worst fears. Hardy notes of this incident 'the greatest misfortune of her life was this feminine loss of courage at the last and critical moment through her estimating her father-in-law by his sons'. Fate also leads her to her meeting with Alec: thus, within a few hours of failing to meet the good preacher, Mr Clare, she meets the false preacher, Alec.**

Pause for *Thought* ❙❙

In what ways do women pay in this phase?

PHASE THE SIXTH *The Convert*

Chapter XLV

Alec chases after Tess and tells her how he was converted by Mr Clare after the death of his mother. Tess pours scorn on his conversion and tells him about the baby. Alec makes her swear upon the Cross-in-Hand not to tempt him.

Commentary: **We see Alec preaching through the narrative perspective of Tess, whose focus is on his face. It has been distorted out of its hereditary shape, a detail that immediately undermines the strength of his conversion. Tess despairs that 'He who had wrought her undoing was now on the side of the Spirit, while she remained unregenerate,' a conclusion that leads her to accuse Alec of merely seeking to secure his 'pleasure in heaven by becoming converted!' This sense of injustice is further emphasised by Hardy's reintroduction of the Garden of Eden motif, with Alec insisting that Tess swears not to tempt him. The fact that the Cross really marks a place where a criminal had been tortured dramatises the chauvinism in Alec's request by reinforcing Tess's own feeling that 'in inhabiting the fleshly tabernacle with which nature had endowed her she was somehow doing wrong'.**

Chapter XLVI

Alec visits Tess while she is working in the fields and asks her to go to Africa with him as his wife. She tells him that she is already married. They are interrupted by Groby, and Alec leaps to her defence. That night Tess writes to Angel declaring her undying affection but revealing a 'monstrous fear'. Alec visits Tess while she is alone and they discuss Angel's doctrinal views. He has missed a preaching engagement to visit her and blames Tess for tempting him.

Commentary: **The chapter opens in realist fashion with an account of hard manual labour, yet the symbolic significance of the slicing-up of phallic objects should not escape us: the problems suffered by Tess derive from men who love her, which is why she prefers Groby, the 'man of stone'. Alec arrives as a 'man in black' to tempt Tess by lifting her 'out of subjection'. It is he, however, who claims to be under temptation, once again invoking the Garden of Eden motif. He, like Angel, defends Tess against Groby and, as Angel will do, offers to take her abroad. The contrived religious discussion brings Angel momentarily back into the narrative: he believes 'in the *spirit* of the Sermon on the Mount', but does not practise its charity. Indeed, it is Alec, though demonstrating contempt for women, who recognises Tess as having 'intrinsic purity in spite of all'. There is, however, as Alec notes, great irony in the fact that Angel's anti-doctrinal views 'might be paving my way back to her'.**

> ### Task 7
>
> Write this scene from Alec's point of view. You need to get some sense of the depth of his conversion and his subsequent inability to deal with the appearance of Tess.

Chapter XLVII

It is March and Tess is working on the punishing steam-driven threshing machine. Alec joins her during her lunch break and renews his suit, informing her that he has lost his faith. She strikes him when he insults Angel, and he responds by telling her that he was her master once, and will be again.

Commentary: **Hardy creates a sense of immediacy by use of the present tense in the opening, which allows him to focus on the way the modern mechanical methods upset the natural rhythms. (We are reminded of the blood-red reaping machine in Chapter XIV). He evokes the Garden of Eden motif, but in the 'hot blackness' of the mechanised Eden it is the 'red tyrant' of steam power (the infernal symbols of black and red converging) that punishes the workers. Tess is under siege from the red tyrant and also Alec, who is the 'blood-red ray in the spectrum of her young life' (p. 42). Tess is selected for special punishment, becoming again a bird in a cage: this will become important later on in her transformation into a defiant sparrow. Tess's striking of Alec demonstrates her brave but futile defiance. Furthermore, her understanding that she is the victim indicates her spiritual ascendancy: she is the victim in the Genesis myth; at the hands of men; in society in general; and of Darwinian and hereditary impulses. Alec's final comment is an interesting statement of patriarchal possession (though she has at least been elevated to the level of lady), which ends, in many ways, with the truth.**

Chapter XLVIII

The threshing continues into the evening and Alec returns for the rat catching. Exhausted by her work, Tess almost breaks down as a more subtle Alec offers to help her family. In a state of despair she writes a passionate appeal to Angel, describing herself as 'exposed to temptation' and begging him to return.

Commentary: **It is ironic that Alec, the biggest rat of all, should evade the hunt and instead pursue Tess at her most vulnerable. As she notes: 'Don't mention my little brothers and sisters — don't make me break down quite!' Yet there is an identifiable softening of her attitude to Alec in this chapter, Tess noting 'perhaps you be a little better and kinder than I have been thinking you were'. The letter offers one of the few times when Tess speaks with her own voice. It emphasises her love for Angel and is full of pathos.**

Chapter XLIX

The letter is sent to Brazil, where Angel lies sick. Experience means that 'he had mentally aged a dozen years' and the words of a dying stranger make him question his treatment of Tess. Meanwhile, Tess learns songs in preparation for his return — but 'Liza-Lu arrives with the news that their mother is dangerously sick.

Commentary: **Timing is crucial in maintaining the tension in the last part of the novel: we know that the letter must arrive quickly, so Hardy slows down the narrative by visiting the stultifying environment of Emminster. We are then offered a flashback of Angel's 'conversion' when he learns that 'the beauty or ugliness of a character lay not only in its achievements, but in its aims and impulses' before returning to the present with Tess's ballad singing. Fate intervenes in the illness of Joan, which reminds us of the help that Alec has just offered.**

Chapter L

Tess returns home to find the family in disarray. Taking over household arrangements, she begins gardening in the family allotment, where she once again meets Alec. She refuses his offer to help the family but is shocked by news of her father's death, an event that means that they will lose the house.

Commentary: **The night-walk takes Tess through a landscape that reflects her own personal history. She passes the field where Angel failed to dance with her; she walks through forests in which white harts had been hunted (medieval symbols of hunted innocence), and witches ducked (reminding us of Alec's accusation of her witch-like charms). Her work in the allotment suggests her rejuvenation of a family gone to seed. Hardy once again invokes the Garden of Eden motif, Alec even acknowledging his role: 'You are Eve, and I am the old Other One come to tempt you…'. The temptation is made unbearable by eviction, which is presented as the next step in their steady hereditary decline.**

Chapter LI

The Durbeyfields are evicted because of their poor reputation, and once again Tess is made to feel responsible for their plight. Alec appears again, offering accommodation at Trantridge, but Tess resists, saying that they have taken rooms in Kingsbere. Tess finally feels that Angel has been unjust and writes him an angry accusatory letter.

Task **8**

What happened to Angel in Brazil and how has his experience changed his attitude to Tess? What do we learn of Tess from her letter (think carefully of the tone)? Is it the convincing voice of a young female farm worker?

❮ Top ten *quotation*

Taking it ➤
Further ➤

Read Hardy's poem 'Tess's Lament' (do an internet search for the title). The poem is told from the point of view of Tess following Angel's departure to Brazil. It emphasises her anguish and builds to the depressing conclusion: 'I cannot bear my fate as writ,/I'd have my life unbe.'

❮ Top ten *quotation*

Pause for *Thought*

Comment on the authorial observation 'By some means the village had to be kept pure.'

Context

Old Lady-Day (6 April), one of the quarter days when rent was due and workers paid, saw rural movement at its greatest, when workers were hired at an annual fair at Dorsetshire. Hardy uses this as a plot device to apply more pressure to his heroine. Her mother falls ill mid-quarter, so that the visit of a sympathetic Tess will in all probability forfeit her wages (Chapter XLIX).

Pause for *Thought*

Who is the convert in this phase?

Commentary: **The chapter opens with social commentary that highlights both Hardy's concern for the break-up of the rural communities and the economic cost of Tess's seduction. The noose is tightening around Tess: the reintroduction of the paint-pot man reminds us of the harsh Christian laws she has broken; gossip isolates her from the local community; the children's innocent faith adds pathos; the legend of the D'Urberville coach reminds us of her hereditary predisposition towards treachery while foreshadowing events of the next phase. She manages, however, still to reject Alec.**

Chapter LII

It is Lady Day, a time of great movement in the agricultural world. Tess meets with Marian and Izz on the road and arrives at Kingsbere to find that their rooms have been let. The family is forced to camp in the churchyard next to the D'Urbervilles' tombs, which Tess wanders off to inspect. Alec surprises her by rising from one of the monuments and continues his suit with confidence. Concerned by what they have observed, Izz and Marian wonder if they can help Tess. A month later they write a letter to Angel.

Commentary: **In this chapter Hardy emphasises the role of hereditary decline. The irony is clear in the fact that, in the home of their ancestors, the Durbeyfields cannot find a home. The prosperity of the ploughman who has taken on Izz and Marian contrasts with the declining fortunes of the Durbeyfields, a point emphasised by Alec's emergence from a tomb with the comment 'The old order changeth. The little finger of the sham D'Urberville can do more for you than the whole dynasty of the real underneath...'. It is the last time that we see Alec. In a remarkably Gothic scene, Tess is left considering suicide.**

PHASE THE SEVENTH *Fulfilment*

Chapter LIII

At Emminster Mr and Mrs Clare are shocked by the sight of their physically emaciated son. He has received Tess's first letter and now reads her second, angry, note. He hesitates to go in search of her and writes instead, receiving a reply from Joan that says that Tess has gone away. He decides to go and find her and, as he packs, the anonymous letter from Izz and Marian reaches him.

Commentary: **Angel has returned a changed man: the harshness of Brazil has taught him that philosophy and theology should give way to love and common humanity. This is a chapter that concerns itself with the written word, whether promises of devotion from Tess or threats from the outside: it encourages us to consider the uneasy relationship between 'truth' and 'happiness'. This is why Joan's reaction is of interest: are we to condemn her for self-interest, or acknowledge that she is simply a mother safeguarding the happiness of her daughter? Hardy cleverly builds up the suspense: we want to know what is happening to Tess but the pace of life at Emminster and the pedestrian exchange of letters leave us unfulfilled.**

Chapter LIV

Angel seeks Tess at Flintcomb-Ash and Marlott, where he learns of the death of John Durbeyfield and pays for his headstone. He is directed to Joan's new home 'in a walled garden'. Initially she is evasive, but eventually takes pity and guides him to Sandbourne.

Commentary: **The return to Marlott sees Angel passing the field where he had refused to dance with Tess. Hardy's interest is in the way in which the significance of such locations in individual human histories fails to translate into wider significance: the birds sing on regardless, and the new tenants of the Durbeyfield house go about their business ignorant of the history of Tess. The inscription 'How are the mighty fallen' reminds us of Tringham's chastening words in Chapter I and also refer to Angel. When Joan claims that they are 'fairly well provided for' we are invited to draw our own conclusions.**

Chapter LV

Angel arrives at Sandbourne and eventually finds Tess in her expensive lodgings. He asks for forgiveness but she, talking like one in a dream, tells him that Alec has won her back. Despite acknowledging her hatred for Alec, she asks Angel to leave.

Commentary: **The setting reveals the changed status of Tess, that she has now been mastered by Alec: the grey-white cashmere of her dressing gown indicating her wealth but also her dubious moral position. Tess is said to withdraw her spirit from her body so that she is left repeating the confused assertion 'too late' without believing it. The speech that passes between them is stilted, summed up by Hardy's observation that 'speech was as**

inexpressive as silence'. She simply repeats observations made by Alec until she returns to an explanation in her 'old fluty pathos'. There is great pathos in Angel's appeals for forgiveness, but even now he does not understand Tess, accusing her of being 'fickle' and attributing her coldness to his emaciated state.

Chapter LVI

Mrs Brooks, the landlady, hears Tess and Angel arguing and then the latter leaves. Later, she notices a red stain on the ceiling and calls a workman to open the door. Alec is found dead and the alarm raised.

Commentary: **The chapter is narrated through the eyes and ears of Mrs Brooks and reads like a police statement. Hardy's careful marshalling of the evidence builds suspense and also disengages us from feelings that would have created a false climax and reflected badly on his heroine. Hardy invokes the ace of hearts symbol to show the inevitability of Alec's murder considering the hand that fate has dealt Tess, and it also reminds us of the death of another 'false Prince', which began the whole tragic course of events.**

Chapter LVII

Angel sets off on foot and is overtaken by Tess, who announces calmly that she has murdered Alec. Angel is not sure whether to believe her, but vows to protect her by every means in his power. They make their way through the back lanes of the countryside until they find a deserted mansion in which to take refuge.

Commentary: **As the marriage of Mercy Chant and Cuthbert is announced, we are guided to find 'fulfilment' in this chapter. The D'Urberville coach makes a last appearance, with Angel acknowledging its validity. In killing Alec, Tess has fulfilled his prophecy that 'I shall die bad.' They find fulfilment in their love, Hardy noting that, despite the magnitude of her crime, 'tenderness was absolutely dominant in Clare at last'. However, there are images of foreboding: the sun's rays pierce the house shutters like a shaft (reminiscent of that which kills Prince) that 'glances' rather than bathes; at the close of the chapter 'they were enveloped in the shades of night which they had no candle to disperse'.**

Taking it **Further**

Compare this climactic scene with the scene from the 1998 television film with Justine Waddell playing Tess: www.youtube.com/ watch?v= Bkkz-WCJDcM

Task 10

Why does Tess kill Alec?

Pause for *Thought*

What is the significance of the fact that this is the first time in the novel that Tess has overtaken somebody on the road?

Chapter LVIII

Tess and Angel spend a happy week in the house, protected by a dense fog. The caretaker finds them sleeping and, though she does not disturb them, they flee northward. They finally come to rest at Stonehenge in the dark. Tess asks Angel to look after 'Liza-Lu. At dawn they are surrounded by police, who respond to Angel's plea by allowing Tess to sleep on. She awakens in the 'growing light' with the words 'I am ready'.

Commentary: **Hardy uses the caretaker of Bramhurst Court to guide the feelings of the reader. We are invited to glimpse the sleeping Angel and Tess through her eyes and her 'momentary sentimentality' at 'their innocent appearance' guides us to a similar feeling. Stonehenge is a fitting destination for Tess's last journey: it is deliberately 'older than the D'Urbervilles' — therefore setting her tragedy against a larger cosmic backdrop. It is an altar for sun worshippers and she is arrested when the sun shines on her while all the rest of the plain is in the shade; and finally she is sacrificed before a group of anonymous men. Tess is fatalistic about death, announcing that 'what must come will come' and 'this happiness could not have lasted...and now I shall not live for you to despise me'. According to the hereditary theme that has run throughout the novel, Tess's insistence on the transference of affection to her sister should come as no surprise. Indeed, Hardy describes 'Liza Lu as 'a spiritualized image of Tess', at the beginning of Chapter LIX.**

Chapter LIX

It is July and Angel and 'Liza-Lu are walking up a hill out of Wintoncester in the early morning. The clock strikes eight and they turn to see a black flag raised, indicating that Tess has been hanged. They pray, and then walk on hand in hand.

Commentary: **The sun shines brightly, emphasising the ambivalence of nature to the fate of Tess. Hardy is heavy-handed in his criticism, invoking 'justice' (note the use of inverted commas) in the form of the 'President of the Immortals'. The classical tragedy reaches its climax with the suggestion that the life of Tess has been fated from the start. As Angel and 'Liza-Lu depart, Hardy invokes Milton's *Paradise Lost*, suggesting that they are the fallen having gained experience from the life of Tess.**

Context

Stonehenge is thought to have been constructed by Pagan Druids as a place where animal and human sacrifices were made at the winter and summer solstices to ensure seasonal renewal and fertility. The word 'henge' is the ancestor of the modern 'hang'; so the death of Tess is foreshadowed.

Task **11**

Two sequences that offer a montage of the whole book are available on YouTube. The choice of image which they have chosen to focus on is significant. Decide which offers the darker interpretation:
www.youtube.com/
watch?v=IR0eM9z0F7A
and
watch?v=Zikn3xYDirw

❮ Top ten *quotation*

Pause for *Thought* ⏸

In what sense is there fulfilment in this last phase?

Themes

Sexual hypocrisy: the 'fallen woman'

Context

The poet Coventry Patmore celebrated the vision of pure womanhood in his highly influential poem *The Angel in the House* (1854), an ideal that was reinforced through a burgeoning periodical literature aimed specifically at women, which limited female horizons to the acquisition of accomplishments (such as needlework and music), capable of establishing a wholesome (a favourite Victorian word) household.

A number of Victorian writers, among them Dickens, Gaskell, George Eliot and Hardy, concerned themselves with the theme of sexual hypocrisy. The Victorian period witnessed the effective neutralising of female sexuality as a combination of Evangelical fervour, royal disgust, stifling adherence to etiquette and repressive patriarchy saw sexual matters retreat from public discourse. As women were straitjacketed in dresses that accentuated a male vision of femininity by removing the erotic, tablecloths were lengthened to avoid arousal at the sight of a naked wooden leg. The desexualised woman was submissive to her husband, a devoted mother and, above all, pure (which is why Hardy's subtitle caused such a fuss). By contrast, the sexualised female was demonised as a 'fallen woman' — an admirably economic term employed to categorise and castigate all those females 'guilty' of having a sexual identity, whether hardened street walker or pregnant teenager. Feminist critics, however, would argue that this interpretation conveniently ignores the fact that the 'mistress' was a staple part of the Victorian nuclear family, allowing the wife to fulfil her role as angelic wife and mother. The concept of the 'fallen woman', therefore, becomes a hypocritical means by which a powerful and neurotic patriarchy could control female sexual behaviour.

Fallen from what, we may ask. Suffice to say it looks beyond a set of arbitrary puritanical standards to Eve's fall from the Garden of Eden, a myth that conveniently places the blame for the very first crime at the feet of a woman. It is perhaps not surprising, therefore, that the Genesis myth is evoked repeatedly in Victorian explorations of the theme of sexual hypocrisy. One excellent example is George Eliot's *Adam Bede* (1859). Set within a pastoral idyll, a young carpenter, naturally named Adam, pursues the local beauty, Hetty. The snake in the grass is the village squire, Arthur Donnithorne, who seduces her before casting her aside. Her sexual 'fall' is compounded by the infanticide of her illegitimate baby. Eliot's is a moral fable: Hetty falls because she is vain and eager for social glamour.

Hardy's exploration of the theme follows the outline of Eliot's cautionary tale, but he does not simply exonerate his heroine: he flings her purity in the face of a Victorian society adhering to hypocritical social taboos. Like Eliot he evokes the myth of the Fall but Hardy's is a post-Darwinian garden, oozing with the sexuality that Victorian society was so eager to suppress. In such a garden, female sexuality is presented as simply part of 'Nature's law' and Tess suffers more than the other milkmaids because of the beauty that makes her the object of continual male harassment. Hardy locates the purity of his Eve in the fact that she struggles against such overwhelming forces for so long. Indeed, he goes one step further, questioning whether the fact that 'she had been made to break a necessary social law, but no law known to the environment' (p. 86) means that she had fallen at all.

If Hardy, like an overprotective father, is keen to vindicate his Eve, then he is savage in his condemnation of the hypocrisy of his Adam and the patriarchal Victorian world that hounds her. Where Hetty finds solace in the church, Tess finds only the harshness of the itinerant sign-painter, the churlishness of the parson for refusing Sorrow a Christian burial, and the limitations of the Evangelical, high church and Comtean traditions displayed by the Clare family. She is let down by her own family, whose shiftlessness is compounded by their encouragement of Tess to use her beauty to secure their own advancement. Furthermore, she is isolated from her village community by the kind of gossiping that eventually sees that she and her family are evicted for her disgrace.

Hardy's biggest target, however, is the power of the hypocritical patriarchy. It is an indictment of male supremacy when Tess announces that she feels safest with farmer Groby, 'that man of stone' (p. 319), who is sincerely unpleasant to her rather than duplicitously pleasant. Alec is a more complex version of George Eliot's Arthur Donnithorne, through whom Hardy is able to condemn an entire class of rich, socially irresponsible and bullying young men, whose hypocrisy extends to finding redemption in an unconvincing conversion. Significantly, both he and Angel continually displace their inability to control their own sexuality on Tess, transforming her into the snake who offers temptation, thus fulfilling the role for women in the Genesis myth. Angel, to some extent, is an entirely new invention: a Victorian 'new man' whose rejection of church dogma in favour of a more liberal humanism seems to provide the appropriate foundation for a more sympathetic response to the plight of Tess. Hardy improves the chances still further by adding the detail of Angel's confession of his own past indiscretions. He proves, however, to be even worse than Alec, and offers the reader a study in the emergence of an ideological humanism that has lost touch with the actual behaviour and frailty of humanity.

Taking it
Further

The popular series of paintings Past and Present (1858) by the artist Augustus Leopold Egg is excellent when considering Tess as a fallen woman. This morality tale shows young women the consequences of infidelity. These images are on the Tate Britain website: www. tate.org.uk. Either type 'Augustus Egg' into the search page or go directly to:

www.tate.org.uk/servlet/ ViewWork?cgroupid=999 999961&workid=4091&se archid=10256

Hardy's late poem
'Heredity' presents this
mysterious power as a
spirit that exists in us all,
the speaker asserting
that 'I am the family face;/
Flesh perishes, I live on'.
The possessor of the face
is therefore turned into
a puppet playing out the
lives of its ancestors. Hardy
explores similar themes in
'The Pedigree', the speaker
exclaiming in despair 'I am
the merest mimicker and
counterfeit! —/Though
thinking, *I am I*.

Top ten *quotation* ❯

Heredity

The theme of heredity is central to the novel, largely because of Hardy's interest in *Essays on Heredity* by the German neo-Darwinian August Weismann. Anticipating modern genetics, Weismann argued for the existence of a 'germ plasm' as the indestructible conveyor of inherited traits and impulses across the generations. It is an idea that seems to have captured the Victorian imagination, largely because it offered a 'spiritualised' mechanism for the transference of acquired characteristics from one generation to the other, which complemented Darwinian theory.

Hardy's exploration of the theme begins with the Durbeyfield family. They are shiftless and morally weak (as demonstrated through their plans to claim kin), but this is to some extent because of a hereditary disposition that leaves them ill equipped to survive in the modern world. In Darwinian terms, their decline is due to their failure to 'adapt' to their environment. To use the botanical metaphor that pervades the book, they represent a fallow period, the ascendant Stoke family actually 'grafting' and adapting the Durbeyfield name for their own. It is therefore fitting that the remnants of the family end up camping in their tomb at Kingsbere, a tomb from which Alec springs with the words 'the old order changeth' (Chapter LII).

It is, however, in relation to Tess that Hardy's use of heredity becomes most noteworthy. Tess's hereditary disposition is traceable in her face; Joan calls it her 'trump card' — it is in fact just the opposite, making her prey to predatory males throughout the novel. It is through its 'fine features' that it is possible to trace her female ancestors whose lineaments were 'so suggestive of merciless treachery' (Chapter XXXIV). This insistence on her lineage transforms Tess into a puppet through which her ancestors continue to live their barbarous lives, and as readers we are invited to consider significant events in the novel, such as her seduction and failure to tell Angel, in the light of her ancestors' record.

If not treacherous, she is certainly proud, impulsive and dreamy — inherited characteristics that lead to morally questionable behaviour. It is, for example, the pride of her chain-mailed ancestors that can be seen in her refusal to ride with Alec to The Slopes, and more dramatically acting through the gauntlet with which she bloodies his nose late in the novel. And just as we are invited to question the absurd pride of John that leads him to make the futile gesture of digging a grave for Prince, we are led to question the proud refusal of Tess to make contact with Angel's family, and also the pride that causes her continually to privilege her own overly refined sense of morality over the need of her siblings.

At other times it is Tess's combination of impulsive and dreamy behaviour that seems questionable. It is because of her dreaminess, for example, that Prince is killed and the family thrown into destitution, and it is in a similar state that she is initially wooed by Alec in the garden of The Slopes. When combined with her impulsiveness, the results are dramatic: it is on impulse that she mounts behind Alec's horse before falling into the state of dreaminess that leads to her seduction; it is on impulse that his murder is carried out, leading to the dreamy honeymoon with Angel. In each case Tess is presented as in the power of forces greater than herself that mould her behaviour. She is both perpetrator and victim, her hereditary disposition offering yet another internal agency against which she must struggle to maintain her own highly refined vision of her purity.

It is only through an understanding of heredity that we can understand Tess's insistence on, and Angel's easy compliance with, the transference of his affections to 'Liza-Lu at the end of the novel. She is 'so good and simple and pure' — the unblemished Tess that he would have got if he had selected her at the Marlott dance. There is, however, less naïve idealisation in Angel's vision now, a characteristic that Hardy dramatises through their departure hand in hand at the end. Hardy's phrasing deliberately echoes the scene in *Paradise Lost* in which Milton describes the ejection of Adam and Eve from the Garden of Eden: thus, they are both fallen and beyond the bounds of Angel's fatal idealisation.

She is both perpetrator and victim

Characters

Tess

Tess dominates the novel to such a degree that the other characters sometimes appear as little more than means by which Hardy can explore his creation. She dominates every scene in which she appears, Hardy noting that 'the eye returns involuntarily to the girl in the pink cotton jacket, she being the most flexuous and finely-drawn figure of them all' (Chapter XIV). We are invited to gaze at her, indeed not so much her as various parts: her bare arms, slender neck and red lips — the latter repeatedly evoked through the loving eyes of both Angel and Alec and, to some extent, Hardy himself. For feminist critics she is the object of male dissection, Hardy the narrator being complicit in this voyeurism. A more charitable view may simply be that he fell in love with his creation and takes a paternal concern in her well-being.

She is guilty of mothering an illegitimate child, of deceit and murder, and yet Hardy provocatively throws her purity in the face of Victorian society, begging the question: in what sense is she a pure woman? In some ways this is not a moral judgement but rather an assertion that she embodies some essence of womanhood. She is, for example, capable of a deep-felt, almost spiritualised, love, Angel at first not comprehending 'the full depth of her devotion, its single-mindedness, its meekness; what long-suffering it guaranteed, what honesty, what endurance, what good faith' (Chapter XXXIII). Furthermore, she exhibits an instinctive sensitivity to the suffering of others, whether the dying pheasants in the woods or her own siblings. This sensitivity, however, is so highly evolved that it is incompatible with the harshness of her environment and instead, as the critic Claire Wright has observed, it feeds her capacity for guilt. She is continually tortured by an exaggerated sense of her own moral responsibility, which is contrasted with her mother's more relaxed way of thinking — the latter is more in harmony with prevailing cultural conditions. This heightened sense of guilt, an internalised version of those external social rules, prevents her from approaching Angel's parents and renders her vulnerable to the emotional blackmail employed by Alec.

Such claims have enraged feminist critics, who take issue with Tess's passivity and victim status: they argue that this is not a woman but

Context

'Tess' is a corruption of 'Teresa'. This was the name of a sixteenth-century Spanish saint of people in need of grace, therefore entirely applicable, who claimed to have seen visions of angels. 'Durbeyfield' is a corruption of the Norman French 'D'Urberville' (itself a corruption since the first letter should be lower case), and indicates the decline of the family from French aristocracy to English peasantry. The debasement of her name recalls the Shakespeare quotation on the title page, 'Poor wounded name'.

a woman created by a male writer. Hardy's Tess, however, is more complex: she is no Lara Croft but she is feisty — she outfoxes Alec on their first ride to The Slopes and later bloodies his lips, and she also harangues the priest for refusing to baptise Sorrow. In such a context her acceptance of Groby's sadistic punishments and Angel's judgement can be seen as stoical and dignified rather than weak. Furthermore, Tess is not simply the victim of male sexuality but is a sexualised individual willing to assert herself. She, in common with the other milkmaids, is depicted as a mere 'portion' of the 'organism called sex' thrust on them by 'cruel Nature's law' (Chapter XXIII). It is this passionate Tess who surprises Angel during their courtship when Hardy notes that 'Clare learnt what an impassioned woman's kisses were like upon the lips of one whom she loved with all her heart and soul' (Chapter XXX).

It is, however, quite clear that Hardy is making a moral claim, one that outraged contemporary society, which equated female purity with virginity. It is this gossipy moral majority that Hardy invokes in his wry observation, following the Durbeyfields' eviction, that 'the village had to be kept pure' (Chapter LI). But, as Hardy continually states, 'it was they that were out of harmony with the actual world, not she' and 'she had been made to break a necessary social law, but no law known to the environment' (Chapter XIII). Hardy questions whether a single act should lead to a lifetime of condemnation, particularly when the woman is clearly the victim of brutish male desire. This is Angel's epiphany in Brazil: 'what Tess had been was of no importance beside what she would be' (Chapter XLIX).

Though Hardy creates a vivid country girl, there is also a sense in which she is symbolic. She is locked into a tragic cycle, which begins with her being dressed in white by her parents before she meets Alec and ends with her being sacrificed on the altar at Stonehenge. In between she is variously a 'visionary essence of womanhood', the 'fallen woman' of Victorian moral censure, and Eve in Hardy's reinvention of the Eden myth. Hardy reinforces this symbolic role by ensnaring her in a web of colour symbols (particularly red) and unfortunate coincidences, such as the confessional letter going astray and Clare's family being absent when she calls.

Alec

Alec is little more than a cardboard cut-out: the moustachioed, cigar-chomping, cane-twirling cad with a 'rolling eye' of Victorian melodrama. He is an outsider in the rural community and is paralleled with artifice:

Task 12

The following front covers all represent Tess and can all be found on the internet. Have a look at them and discuss what each depiction says about the heroine of the novel. Penguin Classics edition, Signet edition, ACT e-library image, Dover Thrift edition, Oxford World Classics edition.

his name is appropriated; he is continually dressing up in different roles — the dandy, the Methodist priest, the labourer; and he is associated with the artificial paradise of The Slopes and Sandbourne. Hardy makes no pretence of developing a complex character: he is a Satanic prince of darkness (continually associated with black) and appeals to Tess's erotic side. From the outset he views her in a sexualised fashion, treating her like a horse that has to be broken and mastered: 'Well, my big Beauty, what can I do for you?' (Chapter V). His seduction of her is entirely physical, though metaphorical — the forceful feeding of strawberries and teaching her to whistle unlocking the sexuality he is able later to exploit in The Chase. As such it is quite clear that he is not without charm, Tess later acknowledging that 'perhaps you be a little better and kinder than I have been thinking you were' (Chapter XLVIII).

The second incarnation of Alec is a slightly more ambiguous figure: although we are guided to find his conversion unconvincing, the way it fractures so conclusively upon the return of Tess indicates the depth of his attachment, a quality that throws into stark relief Angel's abandonment. Although he remains appalling in his pursuit of Tess, using her financial situation and family to break her down, he seems genuinely shocked by the news of Sorrow and at least offers marriage as 'the only reparation I can make for the wrong I did you' (Chapters XLV and XLVI). Furthermore, he is refreshingly honest about his character, acknowledging that 'I was born bad, and I have lived bad, and I shall die bad in all probability' (Chapter XII).

Taking it Further ▶

In Polanski's film of 1980, Alec's sleekly oiled hair and voice, calling Tess 'my pretty', establish him as the villain. How has Polanski presented some of the other characters and what assumptions are we led to make about their characters?

Angel

Angel, like Alec, is an outsider, but he is a theoriser, a 'tentative student of something and everything', 'an intelligence rather than...a man' (Chapters II and XIX). As such he does not fall in love with Tess but idealises her: to him she is 'ethereal to a fault, imaginative to impracticability' (Chapter XXXVI) and she is his 'genuine daughter of Nature', indicating his vision of purity. Indeed, despite his confessed affair and the physical attraction to Tess made manifest by his focus on her lips, he remains a remarkably sexless invention — a character moulded among the starched tablecloths and hymn books of the Emminster vicarage. Hardy cleverly indicates this through his attribution of snake-like qualities to Tess when viewed by Angel on the morning of his proposal: from his perspective, sexual attraction is naughty temptation. Hence his later revulsion when he finds out that Tess is not a virgin and his weak, but entirely accurate, assertion that 'the woman I have been loving is not you' (Chapter XXXV). Hardy's contempt

Top ten quotation ▶

for Angel's behaviour is manifest: he transforms him into a hypocrite through the clumsy inclusion of Angel's own affair, and he also made him a colder character during the evolution from serial to novel.

If Tess is a victim of her hereditary disposition, Angel is a casualty of his religious upbringing. He perceives himself as a thoroughly modern man unshackled by Christian doctrine, but he has simply replaced dogma with equally oppressive humanist ideology. When Tess does not fit in with his vision of her, he reverts to type: the same character trait that led to his rejection of the church, 'a hard logical deposit, like a vein of metal in a soft loam' leads to his rejection of her (Chapter XXXVI). All his former endearments now re-emerge cruelly distorted: she is the 'belated seedling of an effete aristocracy' an 'unapprehending peasant woman' and 'too — childish — unformed — crude' (Chapters XXXV and XXXVI). The shattering of his vision and subsequent mental breakdown, demonstrated by his trying to shock Mercy Chant with his anti-religious bile and his half-hearted invitation to Izz to elope, suggest that Angel's mental balance was always suspect, a fact reinforced by his sudden and comprehensive conversion to Tess in Brazil. His subsequent remorse and return, his spiritual growth being in inverse proportion to his physical decline, offer Hardy's vision of the dangers of mental dislocation from the actual environment.

Neither Alec nor Angel is a particularly credible character, and their main function is twofold: to explore different attitudes *to* Tess and to explore different aspects *of* her character. At its simplest, Alec represents caddish irresponsibility in a patriarchal world in which money assures power and a pretty milkmaid is fair game. Angel offers Hardy an opportunity to criticise two prevalent outlooks: the Romantic tendency to idealise the rural; and also the narrow views of both society and the church.

The two men never appear together, thus reinforcing their symbolic role, which is to appeal to the spiritual and sexual sides of Tess. Initially it seems that Hardy is quite clear in attributing some moral measure to these roles: Angel has a harp and is associated with the sun, while Alec has a fork and is associated with black. Throughout the novel, however, Hardy continually blurs this good/bad symmetry and inverts expectations: both take Tess on cart rides to make proposals to her; both plan to take Tess abroad — one as a missionary, the other as a farmer's wife; both dress her to their idealised taste — Alec as a veritable daughter of nature, while Angel dresses her as a D'Urberville. Furthermore, there is great irony in the fact that Alec is spiritualised through Angel's father and then loses his faith because of Angel's humanism as repeated by Tess, allowing his desire to re-emerge.

❮ Top ten *quotation*

Pause for *Thought* ‖

How does the following critical view enhance your understanding of Angel?

'It is not Angel Clare's fault that he cannot come to Tess when he finds that she has, in his words, been defiled. It is the result of generations of ultra-Christian training, which had left in him an inherent aversion to the female, and to all in himself which pertained to the female...' (D. H. Lawrence, 'A Study of Thomas Hardy', 1936).

Top ten **quotation** ❯

Through such dualities Hardy forces the reader to question, like Angel, 'who was the moral man?' (Chapter XLIX). Furthermore, it is quite clear that, for Hardy, Angel could do with a bit more of Alec's sexuality. Hardy demonstrates this — symbolically: Angel lays his idealised Tess in a tomb next to the D'Urberville mansion with the words 'dead to me', an act that is mirrored by the emergence of Alec from the D'Urberville tomb at Kingsbere later in the novel (Chapters XXXVII and LII). The spiritual must be balanced by the physical: when Angel grasps this fact in Brazil he can then resurrect his love for Tess only by returning Alec to the tomb — for whom there is now no role. Angel's change is captured in Hardy's observation: 'tenderness was absolutely dominant in Clare at last. He kissed her endlessly...' (Chapter LVII).

Angel sleepwalking with Tess to the tomb (as illustrated in 'The Outline of Literature' by J. Drinkwater, 1923)

John Durbeyfield

John is a 'tranter', or dealer, whose drinking, laziness and pride are at the root of the tragedy of Tess. It is he rather than Tess who conjures up Angel's vision of a once proud family turned to fallow. His pride exhibits itself in preposterous ways: the hiring of a coach directly on learning of his lineage; the extravagant burial of Prince; the refusal to allow the vicar to enter the house to baptise Tess's dying baby. Not only does John test Tess's loyalty through his fecklessness, his pride is also part of Tess's hereditary disposition, Hardy noting that she acquiesces to Angel's plan to leave her because of 'her submission — which perhaps was a symptom of that acquiescence in chance too apparent in the whole D'Urberville family' (Chapter XXXVII). (In later editions Hardy placed more emphasis on Tess's pride than on her acquiescence.) Hardy emphasises his irresponsibility by making his death as leaseholder the mechanism that casts Tess out of her home and into the clutches of Alec.

Joan Durbeyfield

Joan, to many critics, is an unsympathetically drawn character who can be blamed directly for her daughter's tragedy due to her desire for self-advancement through a good marriage. Not only does she fail to warn her daughter of the potential dangers, but she blames Tess for falling pregnant without engineering a marriage. When Alec offers help from their financial distress at the end of the novel Joan leaves her in no doubt as to her view with the comment 'what's the use of your playing at marrying gentlemen, if it leaves us like this!' (the plural pregnant with irony) (Chapter LII). Most significantly, her advice concerning the confession is directly contradictory to Tess's own instinct. There are, however, no authorial interventions condemning her behaviour, Hardy remaining ambivalent rather than critical. The reason for this apparent negligence resides in Hardy's observation that:

> **Between the mother, with her fast-perishing lumber of superstitions, folk-lore, dialect, and orally transmitted ballads, and the daughter, with her trained National teachings and Standard knowledge under an infinitely Revised Code, there was a gap of two hundred years as ordinarily understood. When they were together the Jacobean and the Victorian ages were juxtaposed.**
>
> **(Chapter III)**

Joan's values, being of an older and more rural generation, are not measurable by the same means as Tess.

The Clares

The Clares in many ways offer Hardy an opportunity to explore the limitations of religious and middle-class morality. Felix and Cuthbert are particularly insular products of Cambridge theological training: academically isolated, misogynistic and snobbish. Old Mr Clare, who is drawn sympathetically by Hardy, is a sincere Evangelical who may have sprung to help Tess in her hour of need but, although a good man, he is presented as earnest and austere. There is no 'aesthetic, sensuous, pagan pleasure' in his life, instead he peddles a 'renunciative' philosophy (Chapter XXV). As a result of his narrow horizons he is unable to conceive of Tess outside the limited description of the 'virtuous woman'

Task 13

Does Hardy feel that Joan is a bad mother, or that her attitudes are more suited than the overly refined principles of Tess to their harsh environment?

prescribed by the Bible. He, like so many in the novel, lacks the imagination to envisage a real woman outside the compartments of the 'virtuous' and the 'fallen'. Mrs Clare shares her husband's limitations, with a touching concern for Angel's well-being. During his second visit to Emminster, having left Tess, it is she who attempts to comfort Angel by characterising Tess as a pure woman in biblical terms (Chapter XXXIX). Furthermore, we are touched by her anxiety as she waits for her son's return from Brazil.

Rural characters

Context

Wessex was originally a Saxon kingdom, but for Hardy it became the fictitious name, 'partly real, partly dream-country', for that part of England where most of his novels are set.

Hardy's gallery of rural characters helps to evoke his Wessex countryside and explore further different aspects of the character of Tess. Some are simply symbolic, the itinerant sign-painter who makes two entries into the text to demonstrate the harsh doctrinal judgement on Tess's behaviour, and the Amazonian Queens of Spades and Diamonds who contrast with Tess's feminine fragility. Her fellow milkmaids, however, are sensitively drawn, offering parallels with Tess. They all writhe 'feverishly under the oppressiveness of an emotion thrust on them by cruel Nature's law' (Chapter XXIII) and lose out to Tess in the battle for sexual selection. Retty, a pretty descendant from a once great family, turns to suicide, and Marian turns to drink. Thus they demonstrate the resilience of Tess as she is beset by troubles. Marian and Izz, however, do more than this: they also demonstrate the deep-seated morality of the working woman. Both help Tess while at Flintcomb-Ash and take the step of writing to Angel, and Izz turns down her own chance of happiness with Angel with the admission 'nobody could love 'ee more than Tess did!...She would have laid down her life for 'ee' (Chapter XL).

Dairyman Crick stands in opposition to all the other male characters: most obviously, whereas Groby is harsh and tyrannical, Crick exudes the milk of human kindness. In earlier novels, notably *Under the Greenwood Tree* and *The Return of the Native*, Hardy employed a rustic chorus to comment on the unfolding plot, often offering a commonsense and amusing interpretation of the events affecting the protagonists. In *Tess of the D'Urbervilles* Crick fulfils this role, his tales evoking an innocent rural past and oases of humour in the general gloom of the novel. His stories of Jack Dollop being chased by the mother of a girl he had wronged, however, offer more, since they touch so clearly on the condition of Tess. It appears that Tess possesses an exaggerated sense of moral responsibility, which stories like these explode. Country ways, Hardy seems to be implying, where such matters are worked out in a rough and ready manner rather than agonised over, seem to be best.

Form, structure and language

There is a great deal of other material relevant to this section elsewhere in this book. For example, the section on 'Tragedy' (pp. 70–71 of this guide) is 'form', as is the opening part of the 'Critical context' section on serialisation (pp. 71–72). 'Structure' is also covered in activities that invite the 'mapping' of the novel. I have placed 'Symbols and motifs' under the heading of 'Language', but these also help to 'structure' the novel.

Form

Narrative technique

Although, as will be seen in due course, Hardy tells the story of Tess from a variety of different viewpoints, his dominant narrative method is that of the omniscient narrator who tells the story in the third person. Generally it is incorrect to conflate author and narrator, but in this case it is quite clearly Hardy's voice that we hear lambasting various institutions and characters for their treatment of his heroine. His continual interventions are typical of the Victorian novel, Thackeray noting in *Pendennis* (1848–50) that 'in his constant communication with the reader the writer is forced into frankness of expression, and to speak out his own mind and feelings as they urge him...It is a sort of confidential talk between writer and reader'. Thus in Victorian novels the narrator becomes a character in his or her own right, moving in and out of the text and manipulating the reactions of the reader. Generally the narrator's purpose is moral instruction, whether through the earnestness of Gaskell, the intellectualism of Eliot, or the satire or sentimentality of Dickens — for such novelists were keen to raise their work from the level of simple entertainment by establishing it within the context of the mid-Victorian emphasis on self-improvement.

> ...it is quite clearly Hardy's voice that we hear lambasting various institutions and characters for their treatment of his heroine

Hardy's narrative voice

Hardy's moral message in *Tess of the D'Urbervilles* was designed to shock his readers (hence his problems in getting the manuscript published without severe self-censorship) and was delivered less in the tones of a 'confidential conversation' than a public harangue. Part of this process is Hardy's insistence on the authenticity of his story — a real-life tragedy is harder hitting than a fictional account — which he presents as a local history that has been handed to him. He notes, for example, that he is unable to tell us who the girl was who danced with Angel at the club-walking because her name 'has not been handed down' (Chapter II). This sense of verisimilitude is increased by his use of actual local place names and his assumption of some familiarity with them in the minds of his reader, as can be observed in his description of the D'Urberville mansion at Wellbridge as 'so well known to all travellers through the Froom Valley' (Chapter XXXIV). Such detailing is, of course, effective only if he can bring his heroine to life, which he does through such mechanisms as her carefully constructed letter, in addition to detailed observations of her looks, movements and voice. Indeed, it is this last feature, voice being arguably the seat of personal identity, that leads Hardy to his clearest statement with regard to her existence, as he notes that it 'will never be forgotten by those who knew her' (Chapter XIV).

Throughout the narrative Hardy becomes her paternal protector, continually interrupting the text in a hectoring tone to criticise such varying targets as Wordsworth — for his Romantic belief in 'Nature's holy plan'; the hypocrisy of the modern man — articulated in his constant criticism of the idealism underpinning Angel's humanism (Chapter XXXIX); and society in general — for its gossipy narrow-mindedness. A refrain throughout the novel is that 'it was they that were out of harmony with the actual world, not she' (Chapter XIII). In his condemnation of church Hardy is, as might be expected, more cautious, presenting his argument in the third person. When lambasting the orthodoxy of the sign-painter, for example, he carefully removes himself in his suggestion 'Some people might have cried "Alas, poor Theology!" at the hideous defacement — the last grotesque phase of a creed which had served mankind well in its time' (Chapter XII).

A classical rural tale

Hardy, however, was more than simply a polemicist: he had a story to tell and set about it in the most engaging way. Much has been made of Hardy's poor style: criticism has been levelled at his plots, which can appear too contrived and reliant on coincidence — the failure of Angel to find Tess's confessional letter being a good example (Chapter XXXIII); his inconsistent philosophising (he gets into an idealist tangle in the last two paragraphs of Chapter XIII); and his pretentious authorial interventions (an untranslated quotation from Pascal and his claim that Old Mr Clare's 'renunciative philosophy' echoed that of Schopenhauer and Leopardi being particularly excruciating examples (Chapters XXV and XVIII). All are to some extent true: while arguing that coincidence occurs and can effectively demonstrate the action of malign fate, Hardy also admitted that the unique pressures of serial publication caused him to introduce climactic events. Furthermore, his desire not to be labelled a rustic writer combined with some sensitivity to his lack of a university education occasionally led to his being heavy-handed. When employed with a lighter touch, however, Hardy's careful plotting and philosophical speculations allow him to transform a simple country tale into a tragedy of classical proportions. Thus there is a 'cinematic quality' to Hardy's style as we find our point of view moulded by an authorial voice commenting on the wider implications of the actions revealed in the domestic plot.

Hardy's landscapes, however, are never simply stages upon which the domestic drama unfolds, nor are they springboards to metaphysical flights of fancy, but they are brought to us with the minutely observed pen of a poet. Hardy considered himself a 'faithful Wordsworthian', by which he meant that he understood the importance of observing nature closely in order to get to 'the heart of the thing' — he simply rejected the evidence of 'Nature's holy plan' that Wordsworth found there. Hence his interest in recording so minutely the different effects of rain as he does so poetically at the beginning of Chapter XXX, or the 'oozing fatness' of the Var Vale at the beginning of Chapter XXIV, or his attempts to capture the nature of the early morning light that illuminates the courtship of Tess and Angel at Talbothays (Chapter XX).

This careful detailing extends to his characterisation of those who work on the land, characters who are far from the caricatures of farm workers presented in contemporary literature such as Jefferies' *Hodge and His Masters* (1880). Indeed, Hardy uses Angel to disabuse us of the caricature of the 'pitiable dummy known as Hodge', breaking him into 'a number of varied creatures — beings of many minds, beings infinite in difference' (Chapter XVIII). Central to their characterisation is his use of dialect, a feature Hardy addressed in an article in *The Spectator* (1881) in which he stated that he attempted wherever possible to preserve the local idiom and words that have no synonym in Queen's English while

> Hardy… understood the importance of observing nature closely in order to get to 'the heart of the thing'

not compromising the overall sense. Thus, his rural characters add colour and verisimilitude to the narrative, the natural poetry of their dialect becoming part of what the Victorians called a 'rustic chorus' commenting on the main action. Hardy's main focus, however, is on, as he notes in *Tess of the D'Urbervilles*, the 'interesting and better-informed class, ranking distinctly above [them]' (Chapter LI). This is made quite clear in the character of Tess herself, since her schooling means that she speaks with a strong dialect at home but with more received pronunciation abroad and to persons of quality. Her language even alters in the course of the novel as she comes under the influence of Angel. This, however, is not simply a stylistic sop to his middle-class readership but reflects the evolving nature of the rural community: Hardy himself was brought up speaking two languages.

Points of view

Despite Hardy's clear guiding hand throughout the narrative, he often employs a drifting perspective that allows the reader to see certain scenes through the eyes of one of the characters. Through it Hardy is able to explore the engagement of his characters with the world around them. It is quite clear what Tess feels about her family home, for example, because we see it through her eyes and, interestingly, hear it through her ears in the form of the onomatopoeic nick-knock of the cradle (Chapter III). Furthermore, throughout the courtship with Angel, his process of idealisation is demonstrated by Hardy's description of Tess through his eyes, from the 'genuine daughter of Nature' who first enters his consciousness at the breakfast table at Talbothays (Chapter XVIII), to the serpent-like temptress he encounters in the dairy on the morning of his proposal (Chapter XXVII).

Top ten *quotation* ❯

There are other times, however, when Hardy invites us to view his central protagonists through the eyes of minor characters, a process that heightens the sense of their tragic inevitability. When, for example, Tess descends to Trantridge Cross, bedecked in the red of roses and strawberries given to her by Alec, it is through the eyes of her 'fellow-travellers' that we see her. Their 'surprised vision' anticipates the later condemnation of her behaviour, while her embarrassed 'blush' and the blood caused by a rose prick as she discreetly removes it reinforce the web of red imagery that projects her to her tragedy. Similarly, Hardy dramatises Tess's reluctance to return to The Slopes by inviting us to view through the eyes of her distant mother the scene when she is picked up by Alec. Her 'misgiving' is articulated in her physical vacillation, while her mother's irresponsibility is indicated by her

Task *14*

Try rewriting the scene in which Alec invites Tess to ride in his gig from the perspective of either Tess or Alec.

'clapp[ing] her hands like a child' when she mounts beside Alec (Chapter VII).

At other times Hardy uses the perspective of minor characters to detach us from the heightened emotions of the main characters. When Tess murders Alec, for example, Hardy disengages us from feelings that would have reflected badly on his heroine and also creates a false climax by having the whole incident recorded in the form of a witness statement by Mrs Brooks, their landlady (Chapter LVI). Finally, Hardy also uses the observing consciousness of his minor characters to guide our own response. When, for example, we are invited to glimpse the sleeping couple through the eyes of the caretaker of Bramhurst Court, her 'momentary sentimentality' at 'their innocent appearance' guides us to a similar feeling. Its capacity to melt the heart of a stranger suggests that this is their moment of fulfilment (Chapter LVIII).

Structure

Structuring the novel: seasons and setting

Hardy uses both setting and season as a method of structuring the novel. In order to think about this it is useful to try and map the novel out as Hardy structured it.

Phase I: The Maiden

Opens with...News of ancestry (which has a real impact on Tess's future).

Closes with...Alec seducing Tess.

1 **Marlott (Vale of Blackmoor):** Described at beginning of Chapter II as a 'fertile' and beautiful valley, 'a broad rich mass of grass and trees'. It is spring, and we first see Tess at the May-Day dance.

2 **The Slopes:** The setting is beautiful and formal, but artificial — a new house has replaced the old (Chapter V). It is early summer and the fruit here enjoys a premature ripeness. Alec first makes his advances on Tess.

3 **The Chase:** A woodland of 'undoubted primeval date' covered with 'Druidical mistletoe'. It is autumn and Tess is seduced.

Task 15

An excellent way to understand how the narrative is constructed is to transform a short scene into film. Write a screenplay, selecting the most important points of the scene. Include the actors you would choose, music, dialogue and camera angles (low angle shots make the subject important, long shots suggest an ambivalent observer, fade ins and outs can mark time passing).

Task 16

Hardy's Wessex offers an idealisation of his native Dorset. Look at the map on p. xv of the Penguin edition (or find Hardy's own on the website www. st-andrews.ac.uk/~bp10/ wessex/index.shtml) and find those locations that feature in the novel. Tess spends much time on the road; try to trace her walks using the map. Why is Hardy so interested in her journeys?

Phase 2: Maiden no More

Opens with...The pregnancy of Tess.

Closes with...Tess resolving to leave.

1 Marlott: At the end of Chapter 13 Hardy observes: 'At times her whimsical fancy would intensify natural processes around her till they seemed part of her own story.' She emerges from depression into autumn harvest, carrying the harvest of her experiences, Sorrow — her baby. The phase ends, however, with the observation at the end of Chapter 15 that 'a particularly fine spring...moved her, as it moved the wild animals, and made her passionate to go.'

Phase 3: The Rally

Opens with...The descent to Talbothays dairy.

Closes with...Angel's declaration of love.

1 Talbothays: Setting of pastoral beauty, a 'verdant plain' upon which 'milk and butter grew to rankness' such is their profusion. Hardy notes at the beginning of Chapter 16 that Tess 'felt akin to the landscape'. Tess arrives in spring 'full of zest for life' and is wooed in the 'half-compounded, aqueous light which pervaded the open mead' of high summer (Chapter XX).

Phase 4: The Consequence

Opens with...Wedding plans.

Closes with...Tess's confession.

1 Talbothays: the change is very slight as the days draw in and towards their winter marriage. The proposal is eventually accepted 'in the diminishing daylight' and light rain as they deliver the morning milk in a chapter where machinery for the first time breaks into the pastoral idyll. Throughout this period Tess continues to struggle with her conscience.

2 Wellbridge: the 'mouldy old' seat of the D'Urbervilles, with portraits of Tess's ancestors, which suggest a 'merciless treachery'. It is mid-winter when Tess makes her confession.

Phase 5: The Woman Pays

Opens with...Angel rejecting Tess.

Closes with...Tess meeting Alec again.

1 **Wellbridge:** as Tess confesses 'the complexion even of external things seemed to suffer transmutation' as Hardy allows the world to become a reflection of her state of mind. Even the fire seems to laugh at her (Chapter XXXV).

2 **Marlott again:** 'There was no place here for her now' (Chapter XXXVIII).

3 **Flintcomb-Ash:** Winter at what Marian calls 'a starve-acre place' and what Hardy describes as 'sublime in its dreariness'. The name of the farm conjures up the rocky ground in which only hardy crops such as swedes can be grown. Farmer Groby is also a deliberate contrast to farmer Crick. Here the abandoned Tess suffers, her external environment mirroring her internal distress.

4 **Emminster:** 'A quiet vicarage' in mid-winter when luck seems to be against Tess. She arrives when all are at church, but is able to hear Angel's brothers complaining about his marriage.

> ...Tess suffers, her external environment mirroring her internal distress

Phase 6: The Convert

Opens with...Alec pursuing Tess again.

Closes with...Tess weakening.

1 **Flintcomb-Ash:** Alec begins his courtship in winter — a deliberate contrast with the summer at Talbothays. It reaches its climax at the March threshing (Chapter XLVII), a mechanised and destructive contrast to the usual spring vitality. This emerges in part in a hope that Angel will respond to the letter of Tess and join her.

2 **Marlott again:** Tess is plunged into darkness again by the illness of her mother and death of her father. In March Alec appears again to become the Devil in an Eden gone to seed. Old Lady-Day is the season of change in the agricultural world and the Durbeyfield family find themselves evicted.

3 **Kingsbere:** It is April, the season of growth and vitality, and Tess finds herself homeless in the 'half-dead hamlet' that is the D'Urberville ancestral home.

Phase 7: Fulfilment

Opens with...Angel's returning.

Closes with...Execution of Tess.

1 **Sandbourne:** It is a false spring when Angel arrives at the 'fashionable watering-place...like a fairy place suddenly created by the stroke of a wand' (Chapter LV). The setting reveals the changed status of Tess — she has now mastered Alec.

2 **Bramhurst Court:** Angel and Tess find fulfilment amidst the sunshine-filled (Hardy is insistent on the sunshine) 'happy house.' From this point they plunge into the darkness on their final journey.

3 **Stonehenge:** Tess is arrested at dawn in a setting that is deliberately 'older than the D'Urbervilles'. It is a suitable monument to conclude her sacrifice. As she is arrested the sun shines on her while all the rest of the plain is in the shade.

4 **Wintoncaster:** The small redbrick (like the D'Urberville mansion) prison in which Tess is executed. It is July and she dies with 'the sun's rays smiling on piteously'. As he has done throughout the narrative, Hardy now reminds us that nature does not respond to the catastrophes of humankind and, in fact, simply continues its own course.

Language

Symbols and motifs

The D'Urberville coach

Even before we hear of the legend, Hardy is laying foundations. When, for example, John Durbeyfield is first informed of his heritage by Parson Tringham, he immediately hires a coach and interrupts the Marlott dance (which marks the entry of the young village girls into womanhood) with his drunken song claiming lineage with the D'Urbervilles. Thus the curse of her ancestry begins to destroy the hopes of Tess. Indeed, Hardy ensures that the plans of the Durbeyfields to claim kin are always projected in terms of a coach, as they state quite candidly in the Pure Drop: ''tis well to be kin to a coach...and ride in her coach and wear black clothes'. Not only are we aghast at their willingness to prostitute Tess, but the image of the black clothes is ominous.

From this point on Hardy employs the legend of the D'Urberville coach as a symbol of foreboding. It is, for example, one of the many dark omens employed by Hardy during the wedding of Tess and Angel. The fact that Tess feels uneasy at the sight of the hired coach emblazoned with the D'Urberville crest, and the fact that she claims to have seen it previously in a dream, suggest that she has a mysterious connection with the legend that stems from her hereditary disposition (Chapter XXXIII). Angel does not take the legend seriously — he sees it as a quaint rural story connected to an aristocratic privilege that he despises.

However, this changes in Chapter LVII when he grasps the legend and its hereditary implications as the only possible explanation for Tess killing Alec. The fact that Hardy introduces it at this crucial stage of the narrative merely emphasises the fact that, in the eyes of society and according to her own set of moral standards, she is going to commit a crime by marrying Angel.

Hardy also uses the coach in the development of the relationship between Tess and Alec. As he pursues her during her final sojourn at Marlott, his arrival is confused with the sound of the D'Urberville coach, prompting him to narrate more details of the legend. Like Angel, he does not take the legend seriously but he knows more details (doubtless because of his father's research in the British Museum), but he misreads the symbolism, as he does with the Cross-in-Hand and Christianity. His brief summary — 'One of the family is said to have abducted some beautiful woman, who tried to escape from the coach in which he was carrying her off, and in the struggle he killed her — or she killed him — I forget which' — exhibits a carelessness in attribution of blame combined with an ignorance of the irony of his part in capturing and imprisoning a beautiful woman (Chapter LI). For Hardy it adds another symbol of foreboding to the pattern that projects Tess, a real D'Urberville, to her murder of Alec, 'a sham one'.

Birds

Throughout the text Hardy uses bird symbolism for two purposes: to demonstrate his vision of humanity as isolated in an uncaring universe, and to explore the character of Tess. When, for example, Tess descends into the valley of Talbothays Dairy, she is observed to be of no more importance than a 'fly on a billiard-table' (Chapter XVI). Later, as she is doing her early-morning milking she is observed by herons 'moving their heads round in a slow, horizontal, wheel, like the turn of puppets by clockwork' (Chapter XX).

Hardy employs similar imagery when she flees into the garden of Talbothays in a state of utter wretchedness following Dairyman Crick's story of Jack Dollop, which touches on Tess's own tragic history. Here, Hardy notes that 'Only a solitary cracked-voice reed-sparrow greeted her from the bushes by the river, in a sad, machine-made tone, resembling that of a past friend whose friendship she had outworn' (Chapter XXI). Once again Hardy is at pains to remind us that, though it may appear to Tess that the world knows her secret, the universe carries on in its clockwork fashion. Significantly, the sparrow has learned this lesson: his voice is not simply mechanical but has been broken by his existence and

Taking it **Further**

Hardy uses birds throughout his work, generally to reinforce his pessimistic outlook. Read 'The Darkling Thrush' (see victorianweb.org), where Hardy contrasts the joyous song of the bird with the despair of the listener, and 'The Blinded Bird', in which he not only rails against human cruelty, but uses the bird as a metaphor to explore the plight of humanity in a brutal universe.

is 'sad' — a mere echo of the simple Wordsworthian songbirds whose singing suggested the existence of a benevolent God in all nature.

Hardy returns to this theme in his use of the birds that return to Flintcomb-Ash to watch Tess working with Marian in Chapter XLIII. Hardy is at pains to contextualise human suffering within the wider universe with these 'gaunt spectral creatures with tragical eyes — eyes which had witnessed scenes of cataclysmal horror in inaccessible polar regions of a magnitude such as no human being had ever conceived'. Their ghostliness and anonymity suggest that such journeys have been made for millennia, thus adding to the chronological insignificance of Tess and Marian. Furthermore, their 'dumb impassivity' before such suffering suggests that such resignation is the only way to cope with such a harsh universe.

Hardy also employs bird imagery as a means of exploring the character of Tess. It is significant, for example, that in Chapter IX Mrs D'Urberville employs her to whistle to her caged birds, therefore aligning her immediately with animals that are both vulnerable and captive. The employment of Tess, however, takes on greater significance when read in the light of Darwinian theory. Darwin noted in *The Descent of Man* (1871) that birds sing for no other reason than to attract a mate during 'courtship ritual'. Tess, however, has forgotten how to whistle, leaving it to Alec to teach her, thereby metaphorically awakening the primitive sexuality that he will later exploit in the primeval forest of The Chase.

For most of the narrative, however, Hardy employs bird imagery to demonstrate Tess's hunted state. When, for example, she finds herself fleeing the attentions of farmer Groby, she is depicted building a nest in the woods where she is surrounded by dying pheasants, victims of men who 'made it their purpose to destroy life' (Chapter XLI). Interestingly, their plight demonstrates the compassion of Tess, as she immediately forgets her problems to attend to their suffering and finally, in an act full of foreboding, 'she killed the birds tenderly'. This imagery reaches its climax during the threshing in Chapter XLVII when Tess is punished in the 'wire cage' of a machine made by men. As she repulses Alec's advances, splitting his lip with her work gauntlet, Hardy notes how she turned 'up her eyes to him with the hopeless defiance of the sparrow's gaze before its captor twists its neck'. Her resistance is futile, and she knows it. Alec will simply imprison her and other members of the patriarchy will prove the truth of her words as they break her neck at the end of the novel.

Hardy is at pains to contextualise human suffering within the wider universe

Top ten **quotation** ❯

The Garden of Eden

In the beginning, according to Genesis 2:4–3:26, God created Adam and Eve and charged them with tending his garden, commanding them not to eat from the tree of knowledge. Eve, however, is tempted by a serpent, who claims that eating the fruit will turn her into a god capable of knowing the difference between good and evil. She eats and persuades Adam to do so also. When God finds that they have disobeyed his command, he expels them from the garden — so begins man's life of misery. It is a myth that has provided fertile imagery throughout the Western arts for the exploration of male–female relationships and the themes of temptation, guilt and culpability. In a novel in which such themes are foremost, therefore, it is perhaps unsurprising that Hardy employs Edenic imagery as a means of exploring the purity of his heroine.

The innocent Tess first meets Alec in a 'garden', where she accepts the offer of an apple from a devilishly drawn Alec, who then watches her eat it through a 'blue narcotic haze' (Chapter V). To reinforce the point, Hardy terms him the '"tragic mischief" of her drama', but it is clear that her acceptance of the apple ensures that she is 'doomed' to be 'coveted that day by the wrong man'. From this point onwards Edenic imagery is never far from Alec's pursuit of her. Although Alec tempts Tess with a ride home from the Chaseborough dance, she remains pure, refusing to join either Alec or the sexually charged dancers. Her will is broken, however, on the long walk back by a most unusual serpent, in the form of treacle that runs down the back of one of her work colleagues 'like a slimy snake'. Hardy notes that it is her 'misfortune' to be caught laughing at this appearance, a discovery that forces her to seek refuge with Alec. From this moment her fall is assured.

Her fall from what? This is a valid question and one that Hardy spends the rest of the narrative exploring. Fundamentally, Hardy uses her experience to project her into a spiritual superiority to those around her: she has eaten the fruit of the tree of knowledge and 'almost at a leap Tess thus was changed from simple girl to complex woman' who now knows the difference between good and evil. This makes her struggle to resist her love for Angel all the more courageous. Although throughout their idyllic early morning courtship Hardy transforms them into 'Adam and Eve', this sanitised version of nature is very much Angel's perspective, because Tess has already fallen and been expelled from the garden of creationist myth to find herself part of nature governed by laws of Darwinian sexual selection (Chapter XX). Hardy makes this clear in the 'garden scene', where she is drawn to Angel's harp-playing through the

uncultivated portion where the plants smear her with juices, while Angel observes from the cultivated part — his idealised vision of nature. Tess, therefore, remains pure in Hardy's eyes because she acknowledges and struggles against her own desire to maintain her integrity.

The men engage in no such struggle, projecting upon Tess their inability to control their sexual desire. Accordingly, in their eyes Tess is transformed into the snake: on the morning of Angel's proposal Hardy notes how she regarded him as 'Eve at her second waking might have regarded Adam' (the second being significant), while under the 'eyelids [that] hung heavy'

Top ten **quotation** ❭

and the 'coiled-up cable of hair' 'he saw the red interior of her mouth as if it had been a snake's' (Chapter XXVII). Such imagery re-emerges when she tells Angel of her seduction, her 'eyelids drooping down' and her necklace glinting with a 'sinister wink like a toad's' (Chapter XXXIV). Likewise, Alec conveniently blames Tess for his loss of faith, begging her not to tempt him and crying accusingly 'Surely there never was such a maddening mouth since Eve's!...you temptress, Tess' (Chapter XLVI). Alec at least, shorn of his false conversion, acknowledges his role in the fall of Tess, candidly announcing during his second courtship as he stands fork in

Top ten **quotation** ❭

hand in the smoke-filled garden of Marlott, 'this is just like Paradise. You are Eve, and I am the old Other One come to tempt you...' (Chapter L). Once again, however, Tess must be broken before giving in to temptation, which Hardy depicts through events like the threshing, which brings a machine into the garden. In this mechanised 'garden' the threshing machine becomes a 'red tyrant', the black chimney of which runs like a snake 'up beside an ash-tree'. It is a machine that breaks Tess, allowing Hardy to transform Eden into 'Tophet' — a biblical location where children were sacrificed to the god Moloch (Chapter XLVII).

Colours

Throughout the novel Hardy uses colours as a form of narrative signposting designed to show that Tess is caught in a web of inevitability that projects her towards her final tragedy. Some of these relations are quite literally black and white, but Hardy also subverts our expectations in order to draw conclusions regarding the nature of society and the universe.

White

White is used to indicate the purity of Tess. Her birthplace was formerly known as 'the forest of White Hart', in which, according to tradition, a deer spared by Henry VIII was run down and killed: quite clearly Tess is to be the modern quarry (Chapter II). When we first glimpse her dancing at the club she is a picture of virginal innocence, dressed in white and

...Hardy... subverts our expectations in order to draw conclusions regarding... society and the universe

carrying white flowers. Her parents dress her in the same white frock to meet Alec — the preparatory grooming seeming uncomfortably like preparation for a sacrifice (Chapter VII). She is dressed in a white nightgown during the baptism of Sorrow, indicating her purity in Hardy's eyes, and throughout her time at Talbothays (Chapter XIV). The dairy is a world of white presided over by the white-clad Dairyman Crick, whose virtue leads to his at one stage being described as 'miraculously white against a leaden evening sky' (Chapter XXIX). Significantly, Hardy even uses white imagery during the erotically charged garden scene to reinforce the healthiness of Tess's sexual appetite: as the 'snow-white on the apple-tree trunks, made blood-red stains on her skin', it is clear that, although her sexual arousal may be purely at one with nature, it will mark her as an outcast in Victorian society (Chapter XIX). She is also married in white, suggesting that for Hardy this is the act of a pure heart. This purity is emphasised by Hardy's insistence on the 'white margin of the envelope' of her lost confessional note (Chapter XXXIII).

From this point on in the narrative, however, white becomes indicative of absence rather than innocence. Tess's face turns 'sickly white' in response to Angel's harshness on their wedding night (Chapter XXXV). Flintcomb-Ash is, like Talbothays, a world of white — but this time it is the harshness of flint and snow, the white sky offering 'a white vacuity of countenance' that reflects 'Tess's face faded as white as the scene without' (Chapter XLIII). Black becomes dominant in her life: her early morning walks along white roads, a detail indicating the purity of her intentions, are taken in progressively darker clothes, leading to her depiction following her father's death wearing 'a gown bleached by many washings, with a short black jacket over it, the effect of the whole being that of a wedding and funeral guest in one' (Chapter L). It is Alec who becomes her white knight, or as Hardy ironically depicts him, a D'Urberville in a 'white mackintosh' (Chapter LI). When she finally becomes Alec's mistress, she is dressed in a 'cashmere dressing-gown of gray-white' — an indicator of her compromised morality — which is only ended through the murder, which brings together the blood-red imagery with the white of the ceiling (Chapter LV). The spell broken, the lovers are finally brought together, her 'pitiful white smile' meeting 'his white lips' in the washed out moments of fulfilment before death (Chapter LVII).

Black

Black, as might be expected, offers the antithesis to the white imagery described above. Alec is continually associated with blackness, whether it is his tendency throughout the first part of the novel to skulk in the shadows, or his inclination towards mastery present in 'those black

angularities which his face had used to put on when his wishes were thwarted' (Chapter XLV). He darkens Tess' world, she accusing him at one point of 'making the life of such as me bitter and black with sorrow' (Chapter XLV). His legacy casts a shadow over Angel, transforming him on his wedding night into a figure 'black, sinister, and forbidding' against which her figure is merely 'light gray' (Chapter XXXV). As Alec re-enters her life during the threshing at Flintcomb-Ash, Hardy deliberately depicts him as a 'black speck' or 'man in black' associated with the black figure of the hissing, diabolical steam engine (Chapter XLVII). Her last days are shrouded in darkness: her desperate appeal to Angel is penned against the backdrop of her siblings 'all in black frocks' singing 'Here we suffer grief and pain,/Here we meet to part again' — a funeral dirge complemented by the veiled hat with 'black feathers' that she wears immediately after the murder (Chapters LI and LVI). Her death, too, is marked by a 'black flag' (Chapter LIX).

Red

Red is also used by Hardy as a means of ensnaring Tess in a web of tragic determinism. She is distinguished from the other girls at the Marlott dance, for example, by a red ribbon. Angel's missed opportunity projects her into the world of Alec, 'one who stood fair to be the blood-red ray in the spectrum of her young life' (Chapter V).

Red is dominant at The Slopes, from Alec's red mansion, the strawberries that he suggestively feeds to her, and the red berries symbolising his virility (Chapters V and XII). Despite her instinctive reluctance, she is thrown back to him through the red blood of Prince, which splatters her, emphasising her powerlessness in the determined cycle. During her fall, the mechanism through which Alec succeeds is Tess's misfortune to be caught laughing at the sister of the Queen of Diamonds. From this point on, red characterises those external agencies that punish Tess, weakening her capacity to resist his later onslaught: it is the colour of the biblical warnings painted by the itinerant sign-painter, reminding us that she will find no help from the church, only condemnation (Chapter XII); the reaping machine that cuts and scratches her (it also resembles a gallows and is therefore full of foreboding); and the 'red tyrant' of the threshing machine (Chapters XIV and XLVII). Tess's futile resistance to her fate is also symbolised by red: her striking of Alec with a work gauntlet brings 'a scarlet oozing' from his mouth, which links back to the death of Prince (ironically Hardy is parodying him as her knight in a 'white mackintosh' at this

Alec (Jason Flemyng) feeding strawberries to Tess (Justine Waddell) in the 1998 film version

point), and anticipates the 'gigantic ace of hearts' that his blood will form on the ceiling of Mrs Brookes's boarding house. Her execution in a 'red-brick building' is the only possible end since it mirrors the red brick D'Urberville mansion where it all began (Chapter LIX).

Her tragedy, however, does not simply rest on external agencies and accordingly the colour red is also inside Tess, most obviously in the 'deep red lips with keen corners' that attract both Alec and Angel (Chapter XXXIX). Significantly, her mouth when observed from Angel's perspective on the day of his proposal becomes 'the red interior' of 'a snake's', anticipating his shift in focus following the confession. Tess also colours red at moments when she realises that she is trapped into certain actions. Her 'red wrath' emerges when she realises that guilt over the death of Prince will force her to return to Alec, while the economic necessity of marrying Angel brought about by the end of her contract at Talbothays leads to him observing 'I feel the red rising up at her having been caught!' (Chapter XXXII). Interestingly, both she and Angel are bathed in the 'red-coaled glow' of the fire during the confession, imagery that both confirms her determined decline and anticipates his diabolical response.

❮ Top ten *quotation*

Sun rays

Colour imagery works in conjunction with Hardy's use of the sun. The sun shines brightly on her while a girl and during her time at Talbothays, but even here it is noticeable that Angel's wooing takes place in the misty dawn, allowing him to idealise her as a 'genuine daughter of Nature' before the real Tess emerges with the sun (Chapter XVIII). The proposal is accepted on the equinox, from which point there is a gradual darkening in Tess's life: they marry in midwinter, after which she is exiled to the darkness of Flintcomb-Ash. From this point onwards the sun becomes something that punishes Tess, becoming progressively redder as it does so. In the D'Urberville mansion on their wedding night, for example, Hardy notes how 'the sun was so low on that short last afternoon of the year that it shone in through a small opening and formed a golden staff which stretched across to her skirt, where it made a spot like a paint-mark set upon her' (Chapter XXXIV). Not only does its low height in the sky indicate the descent into darkness, but Hardy also evokes the red paint of the itinerant sign-painter. Similar imagery is used at Bramhurst Court, where a partially opened shutter allows a 'shaft of dazzling sunlight' to reveal a bed hung with crimson curtains. Not only are we made aware of the violence of the sunlight but, in evoking the red symbolism, this is clearly where the curtain will come down on the short life of Tess. Significantly, she is executed in broad sunshine, emphasising the ambivalence of the natural world to human suffering (Chapter LIX).

❮ Top ten *quotation*

Taking it ➤ *Further*

There is an excellent essay on this subject by the critic Tony Tanner: 'Colour and Movement in Hardy's Tess of the D'Urbervilles', published in *The Victorian Novel: Essays in Criticism* (1971, ed. Ian Watt).

Contexts

Biographical context

Thomas Hardy was born in Higher Bockhampton, a small village near Dorchester, in 1840. He attended the local village school and Dorsetshire High School and was apprenticed to John Hicks, a local architect, at the age of 16. For the next six years he studied architecture, training that is reflected in the rigid structuring of his plots. During this period he also embarked on a study of literature and the classics, a process of youthful self-improvement that he recounts in his descriptions of the young Jude Fawley in his last novel, *Jude the Obscure* (1895). It is also during this period that Hardy came under the influence of two men who shaped his future development. William Barnes was a poet and chronicler of local events who shared with Hardy a love of the Dorsetshire countryside, its labourers and their fast-disappearing dialect and customs. Horace Moule (the model for Angel Clare) was a parson's son who introduced him to the work of contemporary humanist philosophers.

In 1862 Hardy moved to London where he became a practising architect of some distinction. Living in London brought him into contact with a modern cosmopolitan culture that was questioning the old religious and scientific certainties. Ill health made him return to Hicks in 1867, but it was a young Hardy fired with ambition to be a writer. His first novel, a satire of class called *The Poor Man and the Lady*, was unpublished but his second, *Desperate Remedies* (1871), a melodrama in the style of Wilkie Collins, was published at Hardy's own expense. The demoralising effect of its poor reception was partly offset by his falling in love with Emma Gifford, the daughter of a parson in St Juliot upon whose church Hardy was architecturally engaged (the courtship is recounted in his 1873 novel *A Pair of Blue Eyes*). His novel *Under the Greenwood Tree* was more successful when it was published in 1872, and *Far From the Madding Crowd* (1874) proved such a success that he was able to give up architecture and devote himself to writing full-time.

Hardy and Emma married but it was not a happy marriage, Emma becoming increasingly reclusive as her husband, who could be coldly insensitive, became more successful. Upon her death in 1912 Hardy expunged his guilt with an outpouring of lyrical poetry that captured the happiness and gradual cooling of their love. Between 1878, with the publication of *The Return of the Native*, and 1895, Hardy enjoyed great success as a novelist. Following the success of his earlier 'pastoral novels', however, Hardy's desire not to be labelled a rural writer meant that he often pushed the limits of Victorian middle-class tolerance (*Tess of the D'Urbervilles* is typical in this respect). Such was the moral outcry after the publication of *Jude the Obscure*, however, that he turned away from prose to concentrate on poetry until his death in 1928. He married Florence Dugdale in 1912 and, anxious about his reputation, set about destroying his letters and journals while writing an autobiography that he passed off as the work of Florence. Such was his success in this, that the creation of *The Life of Thomas Hardy* can be considered his last true work of fiction.

Taking it ➤
Further ➤

A useful gallery has been put together on the Victorian web by Philip V. Allingham: www. victorianweb.org/authors/ (click on 'Thomas Hardy', then 'Visual Arts'). Here there are slide shows with pictures pertinent to Hardy (e.g. place of birth, school, and locations important in his novels).

Historical context

Rural England

Hardy's great novels are set in his rural Dorsetshire and reflect the life of those who acknowledged that he was the recorder of fast disappearing traditions, values, dialects and people. His novels reflect great change, as the once static, rural community was thrown into a state of instability and mobility.

Historian and novelist

The aims of the historian and novelist are to some degree in conflict: the cold objectivity of the former can deaden while the reviving breath of the writer of fiction can bring sentimentality and caricature. The 1880s saw a proliferation of the latter, typified by Richard Jefferies's *Hodge and His Masters* (1880), as the urban middle classes sought a window on the rural world. Hardy, of course, is not immune to such sentimentality, the very titles of his early works *Under the Greenwood Tree* (1872) and *Far From the Madding Crowd* (1874) announcing their pastoral roots, but he is more even-handed in his treatment of the agricultural world. Indeed, it was to dispel the sentimental vision of nature that Hardy published his essay *The Dorsetshire Labourer* (1883). He is not nostalgic, and acknowledges the substantial improvements in the living conditions of

workers. Nevertheless, the general tendency is to regret the passing of a way of life in which rural workers were in touch with the land, their community and an ancient set of values.

This even-handedness is present in *Tess of the D'Urbervilles*. Throughout the novel there is something noble, even religious, in humanity's close relationship with nature — a spirituality that precedes and outlasts the established church, a sentiment that is captured in his observation that 'the mill still worked on, food being a perennial necessity; the abbey had perished, creeds being transient' (Chapter XXXV). Unlike Angel Clare, however, Hardy was no simple idealist: the milkmaids, who enjoy the pastoral idyll of Talbothays, suffer on Flintcomb-Ash, inoculating themselves against the pain with drink. Economic necessity has taken the place of rural rhythms — they work while wet through because 'if they did not work they would not get paid'. And yet Hardy finds in their plight a certain nobility, observing that working in such conditions 'demands a distinct modicum of stoicism, even valour' (Chapter XLIII).

Machines in the garden

Hardy's novels span the period when a number of labour-intensive agricultural activities became mechanised, a transformation he greeted with scepticism. In *The Mayor of Casterbridge* (1886), for example, the innovative seed drill replaces the older method of broadcasting seed by hand, leading Hardy to note regretfully that 'the romance of the sower is gone for good'. Machines such as the threshing machine that we see in the novel were generally encouraged by farmers, who found them economically efficient, and resisted by workers, whose labour they replaced. Such machines upset the former agricultural rhythms, which had been dependent on season, weather and the speed of man or animal: with the advent of steam power, workers were rushing to keep pace with the machine. Furthermore, such machines replaced winter work and therefore depressed wages and created unemployment. Rural unrest at such industrial practices reached its height in the 'Swing riots' in the 1830s, when machines and farms were burnt by the Robin Hood figure of 'Captain Swing' and his associates.

Rural mobility

A combination of the railway (which enabled people to travel longer distances), unemployment (due to mechanisation), casualisation of labour (due to seasonal demand), compulsory education (which left children unavailable for farm labour and broadened their horizons) and simple ambition meant that the greatest change observed by Hardy during his lifetime was the increase in rural mobility. This process was accelerated by the breakdown of the old family tenant farms — those families who, according to Hardy, 'formed the backbone of the village life in the past' (Chapter LI). Thus, labourers were constantly on the road looking for work. Movement in Hardy's work, however, does not simply entail walking to a new farm, it also embraces emigration. One of the key British exports of the Victorian period was its people: it solved penal and unemployment problems at home while solidifying the Empire. For Hardy, in novels such as *Far From the Madding Crowd* and *The Mayor of Casterbridge*, emigration tends to be a symbol signifying both the dissatisfaction and dreamy ambition of some of his central characters. This is its function in *Tess of the D'Urbervilles*: but Angel actually goes to Brazil 'in common with all the English farmers and farm-labourers who, just at this time, were deluded into going hither by promises of the Brazilian Government' (Chapter XLI). Within the novel the hardship of Brazil acts as a mechanism for Angel's revelation and acceptance of Tess, but also emphasises Hardy's Darwinian belief in the necessity of adaptation and the survival of the fittest. Angel's fellow farmers are strong men but are unable to adapt to 'the weathers by which they were surprised on Brazilian plains' and accordingly they suffer and die (Chapter XLI).

Social context

Religion

The nineteenth century was a period of great religious upheaval in which established beliefs found themselves undermined by the assault of utilitarianism (the humanist system popularised by Jeremy Bentham, predicated on the principle of the greatest happiness for the greatest number), German biblical scholarship (which treated the Bible as a historical document rather than God's word) and scientific study. Hammer blows were struck by highly influential books such as *Essays and Reviews* (1860), which sought to treat Christ as a historical figure; Lyell's *Antiquity of Man* (1863), which posited a world older than that suggested in the Genesis myth; and Darwin's *Descent of Man* (1871), which first hypothesised on man's descent from the ape. Paradoxically, perhaps, one result of such assaults was an upsurge in religious activity:

it was a period of religious movements as the Broad Church (the established Anglican Church) split into different factions seeking alternative means of adapting to the new conditions. The largest of these was the Evangelical movement, which proved very popular among the working classes as it offered a morally earnest attempt to bring religion back to the people, unmediated by the established church. At the other end of the religious spectrum the universities spawned the high church Tractarian movement, which argued that the ceremony and ritual of the church was at the very heart of belief.

Hardy, who once considered training for the church, was alive to these shifts in the spiritual life of the nation, and explored them throughout his work. For example, the distinction between faith and the way it is organised through religion is emphasised in the novels and poems by Hardy's evocation of a Wessex landscape with customs that predate Christianity. He sets all the action of *The Return of the Native*, for example, on Egdon Heath, an ancient elemental stretch of land whose pagan burial sites and customs mould the beliefs of the contemporary dwellers. They are not atheists, but their spiritual lives are not simply confined to Christian practices, and their belief manifests itself in a number of pagan ceremonies. Hardy's thinking here was influenced by the writing of the political philosopher John Stuart Mill, particularly his *On Liberty*, and Arnold's *Culture and Anarchy*, which sought to exalt Hellenism (classical culture) at the expense of Hebraism (Christianity). In Hardy's later novels the energy and spirit of the pagan world is continually contrasted with a Christian world of repression. In *Jude the Obscure*, for example, Sue Bridehead continually characterises Christianity as a faith encoded in 'thou shalt not', seeing her sexual liberation with Jude as a return 'to Greek joyousness', before she is punished for it.

Anti-Christian sentiment

It is quite clear that the orthodox Christianity with which we are presented in *Tess of the D'Urbervilles* has little to recommend it. During her darkest hours Tess finds no help from the church: the itinerant sign-painter offers merely a creed of abstinence and punishment, 'the last grotesque phase of a creed which had served mankind well'; her attempts to find solace in a church service are met with a gossiping band of parochialism, Hardy noting that 'it was they that were out of harmony with nature not Tess'; and finally we are guided to sympathy for Tess's home-baptism, and indeed the behaviour of the whole community, in seeking to bury their infants in consecrated ground.

Hardy reserves his harshest criticism, however, for the Clare family — the kind of family that should have helped Tess, but which ends up destroying her. Through his depiction of Felix and Cuthbert, Hardy criticises the high church. They are particularly insular products of Cambridge theological training that 'candidly recognized that there were a few unimportant scores of millions of outsiders in civilized society, persons who were neither University men nor churchmen; but they were to be tolerated rather than reckoned with and respected' (Chapter XXV). Academically isolated, misogynistic, snobbish, they are 'super-fine clerics' who have mistaken common humanity for theology.

Evangelicalism

Old Mr Clare, the 'Evangelical of the Evangelicals', is presented as a good man (who may have sprung to help Tess in her hour of need), but earnest and austere with no hint of the 'aesthetic, sensuous, pagan pleasure'. As a result of his limited horizons he is unable to conceive of Tess outside the limited description of the 'virtuous woman' prescribed by the Bible: he, like so many in the novel, lacks the imagination to envisage a real woman outside the compartments of the virtuous and the fallen. The emptiness of Clare's Evangelicalism is exemplified in the conversion of Alec. Tess seems to articulate the views of Hardy in her scornful dismissal of those who 'take your fill of pleasure on earth by making the life of such as me bitter and black...when you have had enough of that, to think of securing your pleasure in heaven by becoming converted!' Hardy emphasises the injustice further by having Alec mistake the Cross in Hand (a place where wrongdoers were punished) for the 'devotional cross' and making Tess swear on oath not to allow her beauty to tempt him: symbolically, in the eyes of the church, she must be punished.

Positivism: the religion of humanity

Another aspect of religion explored in the novel is that of positivism, a secular alternative to Christianity, complete with saints and priests, developed by the French philosopher Auguste Comte in the early nineteenth century. Positivism promised to replace God with a scientific understanding of humankind. To achieve this accommodation, however, society must evolve through three distinct phases: the theological (in which the unknown is explained through recourse to God), the metaphysical (which explains the unknown through more general systems and theories), and the positive (which understands the scientific laws underpinning the universe). The contemporary positivist thinker Frederic Harrison described *Tess of the D'Urbervilles* as 'a positivist

allegory symbolic work in which characters and events represent a deeper political, historical or moral meaning

allegory or sermon', in which Angel acts as a positivist priest, easing Tess from her primitive theological beliefs to a higher level. Tess, in common with the other milkmaids, is described as being at the primitive theological stage, with beliefs that are 'essentially polytheistic'. Angel admires the sincerity of such views, but looks forward to 'an ethical system without any dogma' (Chapter XLVII) in which 'moral and intellectual training would appreciably, perhaps considerably, elevate... human nature' (Chapter XXVI). In guiding her to this goal he becomes her priest, so that in times of trouble we are told that 'she tried to pray to God, but it was her husband who really had her supplication' (Chapter XXXIII).

Angel's limitations, however, indicate that Hardy was as weary of positivism as of organised religion: in both *The Return of the Native* and *Tess of the D'Urbervilles* he warns of the dangers inherent in simply replacing one idealistic creed with another. Though he considers himself a humanist, Angel lacks common humanity and remains as insular as his brothers. It is the idealised Tess, 'a genuine child of nature', who becomes the focus of his positivist idolatry, which is why his reaction to her seduction is so disproportionate. It takes the suffering of Brazil to make him question 'all the reasoned ethics of the philosophers' and reassess his own parochialism. A strain of pity for the pain endured by humankind now tempers the 'iron' of his ethical standards, together with an acknowledgement that the moral potential of Tess is more important than her past deeds.

Cultural context

Darwinism

In the early part of the nineteenth century, to take a walk with William Wordsworth among the bobbing daffodils was to experience the majesty of nature shaped for man's delight by a benevolent God. It was a poetic position vindicated by science, as works such as William Paley's *Natural Theology* (1802) and the collection of essays making up the *Bridgewater Treatises* (1833) employed contemporary discoveries in geology, astronomy and biology to provide evidence of God's presence in nature. Challenging this current, however, were the evolutionists, men like Erasmus Darwin (father of Charles) who began to question whether the world had in fact remained static since the times of Genesis. Such views, however, remained marginal until the 1850s when Charles Darwin published his *The Origin of Species* (1859). It was a truly revolutionary book because it removed the need for God in the universe, replacing him with the simple principle of 'natural selection', according to which, species are governed by the impulse to feed, procreate and dominate competitors. Overnight, nature was transformed from proof of God's grandeur to a savage 'struggle for existence' in which the most successful may not be the best but simply those best adapted to their environment.

Hardy was only 19 when *The Origin of Species* appeared and it shaped his views concerning nature. Hardy's landscape is rarely a rural idyll. Most often it echoes to the pain of those species caught up in the struggle for survival. Tess, for example, is described by Angel as a 'genuine daughter of Nature', an observation pregnant with irony in the post-Darwinian world. On one level, this highlights her connection with hunted animals, most notably the white hart of Blackmoor legend, and a variety of birds. On another, it relates to her 'natural' sexual appetites. Such is the suffering of characters such as Izz Huett. What makes that experienced by Tess so much greater is that Hardy extrapolated from Darwin 'the woeful fact [that] the human race is too extremely developed for its corporeal conditions'. In essence, Tess has evolved an excessive sensitivity to her environment, which sets her apart from the community represented by her mother. The damaging consequences of this sensitivity are demonstrated most clearly by Hardy through his representation of the activity of falling in love, which becomes an experience to be endured rather than enjoyed.

❰ Top ten *quotation*

Falling in love the Hardy way

The Darwinian theory of 'sexual selection' reduces love to the need of the species to reproduce itself, acting through the unconscious individual. Two features of the theory interested Hardy: the way individuals might become victims of their sexual impulse, and the disastrous consequences of selecting a partner based on such primitive urges. Together they form an overarching plot device in a great deal of his fiction: his characters are continually struggling to control their primitive sexuality, which often leads to their becoming prey to unscrupulous lovers. In *Far From the Madding Crowd*, for example, the growing affection between Bathsheba Everdene and the shepherd Gabriel Oak is shattered by the arrival of dashing Sergeant Troy. In a particularly Hardyan scene, Troy arouses her sexual nature through his sword display, which acts as a form of Darwinian 'courtship ritual'. The scene has its corollary in the Marlott dance (a fertility ritual marking the passage to sexual maturity), which opens *Tess of the D'Urbervilles*. Here,

the young Tess is too sensitive to be assertive and remains unselected by Angel Clare, with disastrous consequences.

It is left to Alec to awaken her sexuality, which he does by teaching her to whistle. Darwin noted in *The Descent of Man* (1871) that birds sing to attract a mate during 'courtship ritual'. Tess, however, has forgotten how to whistle, leaving it to Alec to teach her, thereby metaphorically awakening the sexuality that he will later exploit. Significantly, Tess's seduction is shrouded in a haze of sleepiness, when she is least equipped to fend off his advances and also control her own sexual nature. It is this instinct that is re-awakened in the garden of Talbothays Dairy by Angel's harp. Here, his notes mingle with the 'mists of pollen', drawing Tess towards him through the uncultivated portion of the garden where she is adorned with juices and stains that affirm her as part of a wilder Darwinian nature. Angel remains in the cultivated portion, which allows him to sanctify her as a 'new-sprung child of nature': she is — but not the nature that convinced Wordsworth of the existence of a holy plan, rather she is of the harsh nature that he will find in Brazil.

Pessimism

Hardy's work has frequently been described as pessimistic, but in the last quarter of the nineteenth century such an outlook was not unusual. Mass urbanisation, an acknowledgement of the horrors of the industrial revolution, and the fear, caused by German biblical scholarship, that humankind may be alone in a meaningless universe, had led to the collapse of the optimism that defined the Romantic movement of the early part of the century. This pessimism is reflected in the work of a number of contemporary authors — particularly Charles Dickens and Elizabeth Gaskell, who sought to expose the inhumanity of capitalist industrialisation. Gaskell's *Mary Barton* (1848) and *North and South* (1855) focus on the poverty and despair of those caught up in the factory life in Manchester. Dickens follows similar critical lines in *Hard Times* (1854). Throughout his writing career, Hardy was also critical of the society in which he lived: in *The Woodlanders*, for example, he rails against the unjust marriage laws; in *Jude the Obscure* his target is the elite university system; in *The Mayor of Casterbridge* his interest is the breakdown of the rural economy; and in *Tess of the D'Urbervilles* Hardy is at pains to expose the irresponsibility of male sexual behaviour and the hypocrisy of Victorian society. Hardy's gloomy view of the human condition, however, is not simply the product of social inequality, but rather his belief that contemporary science and philosophy were discovering that human existence was utterly meaningless.

Following his loss of faith in the mid-1860s, Hardy began to conceive of a godless world governed by determining laws, the cold universe feared by Tennyson in his 'In Memoriam' (1850). Instead of Wordsworth's 'holy plan' — something he attacks directly in *Tess of the D'Urbervilles* — the behaviour of man is determined by harsh deterministic laws. What makes the life of a character like Tess so intolerable, however, is that she has evolved more quickly then her immediate environment, and developed sensitivity to its harshness. From the very beginning Hardy is at pains to stress that Tess is dislocated from her environment: she has evolved 200 years beyond the rural ways of her mother (even speaking a different language), and suffers the 'unspeakable dreariness' of the Malthusian nightmare of her family home. Crucially, Tess seems to have some inkling that things are not as they should be, but her unhappiness derives not only from what happens to her but rather from her intuitive grasp of the futility of life. It is as a young girl that she makes the observation to Abraham that we live on a 'blighted' planet (Chapter IV), and later that she articulates her despair in terms of seeing 'numbers of to-morrows just all in a line...but they all seem very fierce and cruel and as if they said, "I'm coming! Beware o' me! Beware o' me!"...' (Chapter XIX). Hardy helpfully informs us in an authorial comment that what his heroine is trying to express in her 'own native phrases' is a feeling shared by many contemporaries, which might be termed 'the ache of modernism': a general questioning of the point of existence.

> **Context**
>
> The spectre of the influential political economist, the Reverend Thomas Malthus (1766–1834) — who argued that population naturally tended to increase faster than food supply, hence poverty and starvation could only get worse — continued to darken Victorian attitudes to family planning and poor relief right to the end of the century.

❰ Top ten *quotation*

Literary context

Pastoralism

Pastoralism as a genre usually refers to a poem or piece of prose set in an idealised nature in which shepherds and shepherdesses lead a simple rustic life. It offers a vehicle for moral and social criticism, in which the country life is compared favourably with the corrupting influence of the urban life, and often relies on allegory. It has its roots in the ancient Greek pastorals but has been reinvented throughout various literary and artistic periods. In Elizabethan and Jacobean England the image of forlorn shepherds serenading their loved ones became a staple, Shakespeare exploring the genre in the plays *As You Like It* (1590) and

A Winter's Tale (1610). In the Victorian period the pastoral tradition was eclipsed by the urban novel, though it does emerge in the early novels of George Eliot: her *Adam Bede* (1859), however, offers a jaundiced account (see 'Sexual hypocrisy' in the *Themes* section).

This is the tradition into which Hardy slides, the titles of his first two novels *Under the Greenwood Tree* (1872) and *Far From the Madding Crowd* (1874) evoking a pastoral literature (the first is a song in *As You Like It* and the latter a line from Gray's 'Elegy in a Country Churchyard'), which he later subverts. Both are peopled with suitably rustic characters and contain sympathetically observed farming practices, but the underlying theme is one of harshness. Hardy's retreat from the pastoral was hastened by Darwin's publication of *The Origin of Species* (1859), which transformed the rural idyll into a battleground for competing species (see 'Darwinism' earlier in this section (pp. 64–66)). We see this paradoxical presentation of nature in *Tess of the D'Urbervilles*. Tess is as close as Hardy comes to creating an innocent pastoral girl. He emphasises her affinity with nature by using pathetic fallacy to reflect her moods (such as her descent into Talbothays, Chapter XVI) and employing various natural symbols, such as the sun, the white hart and a variety of different birds, to reflect her vulnerability. However, she is also a convincingly drawn working woman born into poverty and ground down by a variety of farming machines. Furthermore, Hardy's nature is not the sanitised version of Arcadian myth but a Darwinian struggle for sexual selection in which Tess, in common with the other milkmaids, 'writhes feverishly' under the oppressiveness of 'cruel Nature's law'. By bringing together the real and the ideal, the critic Ronald Draper argues, Hardy sets out in the novel to demonstrate the corrupting effect of the ideal. It is, therefore, both pastoral and anti-pastoral: evoking the genre to criticise its inherent idealism.

Taking it *Further* ▶

Hardy evokes this new pastoralism in the poem 'In a Wood' in which the speaker is a city dweller who turns to the wood for 'sylvan peace' only to be horrified by the struggle for existence that he finds. Hardy pursues this theme further in his novel *The Woodlanders* (1887), the superficially idyllic lives of the inhabitants of the Hintock woods masking the continuous romantic struggles of the central characters.

© Illustrated London News Ltd/Mary Evans

Tess's affinity with nature is apparent in this 1891 illustration of Tess flinging herself on the ground and considering her future

Realism

Realism refers to a literary genre pop[...] [...]eteenth-century France, America and Britain, which aimed to rep[...]ent the world as it was, without the flights of fancy associated with romantic literature. George Eliot's *Middlemarch* (1871–72) provides a good example, presenting to the reader what purports to be a faithful account of provincial life. Many realist novelists chose to focus on the lives of the lower classes, notable examples being Elizabeth Gaskell's *Mary Barton* (1848) and Charles Dickens' *Hard Times* (1854), which sought to give a faithful account of the poverty suffered by those working in the industrial revolution.

Naturalism is a late-nineteenth-century form of realism, associated with the French novelist Emile Zola. In such fiction events are recorded faithfully according to the principles of realism, but presented in such a way that they reveal something of the larger nature of reality. More specifically, it encouraged writers to show how characters are determined by environmental forces and internal stresses that they neither understand nor can control.

Tess of the D'Urbervilles exhibits realist and naturalist traits rather than a full agenda. To begin with, unlike the works of Dickens and Gaskell, Hardy is interested in the rural, rather than the urban, poor. This can be seen quite clearly in his depiction of the Malthusian nightmare of the Durbeyfield home, the dissolution of the other milkmaids Izz and Retty, and the working conditions at Flintcomb-Ash. Tess herself, with her natural paganism and 'standard English' vying with her Dorset dialect, is in so many ways a realistic representation of an English field woman.

Such descriptions are typical of Zola (with whom Hardy has been linked), not only because they focus on rural poverty, but because such conditions are crucial to moulding the behaviour of the central characters. Although he refuted Zola's call to transform the novel into a laboratory experiment in order to demonstrate how character is developed by environment, it is quite clear that Hardy's novels of 'character and environment' do just this. Indeed, his tendency to link the behaviour of Tess with wider motivating forces makes the novel, to some extent, his naturalistic masterpiece. At its simplest, the forces that mould her life are represented by the seasons and the geographical locations in which she finds herself. More particularly, she is encumbered by a variety of Darwinian and hereditary impulses that are expressed in a number of carefully crafted scenes that demonstrate these forces at work. Hardy is, however, far too interested in his creation to let her develop in the organic way counselled by Zola. He eschews authorial objectivity

and is continually interfering in the narrative, drawing moral conclusions and ensnaring her in a web of symbolism to project her towards her denouement. The novel's realism, therefore, is idiosyncratic rather than doctrinaire, part of a jumble of competing literary genres that defy a single narrative force.

Tragedy

The term 'tragedy' has become so ubiquitous that it has come to refer to anything that seems disastrous. In its strict sense, however, a tragedy is a drama in verse or prose that conforms to a series of rules established by the great Greek tragedians and codified in Aristotle's *Poetics*. Put simply, a tragedy must show the plight of one of noble birth who is brought to catastrophe by the actions of the gods, who use the Fates to exploit a flaw (hamartia) in his otherwise impeccable character. The purpose of such a tale was to arouse pity and fear and thus produce a catharsis of these emotions in the audience. The basic structure is refined further by the introduction of the unities of action, time and place, which encouraged writers to focus on a central character without subplots and develop the action according to an identifiable timescale (within a day or a year) and in a single location. This basic model has been reinvented through the ages, medieval tragedy introducing the idea of the 'wheel of fortune', in which a blindfolded 'Dame Fortune' turned the wheel at whim, and Shakespeare replacing the Fates with other external agencies.

Hardy, in common with a number of Victorian writers, had a great interest in the Greek tragic tradition. In *Tess of the D'Urbervilles,* this is made clear through his descriptions of the Wessex landscape. Many locations may refer to places locatable on a map — Tess is seduced in the oldest wood in England; wooed in the Arcadia of Talbothay's; and punished in the barrenness of Flintcomb-Ash — but they are highly idealised. It is a landscape that not only charts her decline but also reminds us of her insignificance, both geographically — she is compared to a fly on a billiard-table — and chronologically. Furthermore, the narrative resonates with festivals such as the 'club-walking', which connect the inhabitants to their pagan past.

It is, however, when we consider Tess herself that Hardy's tragic ambitions become clear. Hardy jotted in *The Life* with regard to the novel that 'the best tragedy — highest tragedy in short — is that of the WORTHY encompassed by the INEVITABLE'. As Hardy's knowingly provocative subtitle suggests, Tess is a 'pure woman' assailed by forces beyond her control against which she must struggle to maintain her own sense of virtue. Indeed, the struggle is vital: if she had been Izz Huett and had given herself up to Angel unquestioningly, then there would be no tragedy. At its simplest level the novel is a 'social tragedy' in which she is condemned for a social crime (having sex outside marriage) by a patriarchal and hypocritical society. Throughout, Hardy is at pains to stress her worthiness in contrast to those surrounding her: her feckless father, the bullying Alec, the harshly doctrinal church and the priggish Angel. He goes further, however, to question whether Tess's perceived 'crime' deserves any condemnation at all. Two years before publication Hardy noted 'that which, socially, is a great tragedy may be in Nature no alarming circumstance', a sentiment that informs his defence of Tess in that 'she had been made to break a necessary social law, but no law known to the environment' (Chapter XIII). It is, he argues, her potential rather than her past that is of more importance.

What makes the novel more than simply a 'social tragedy', however, is Hardy's focus on the character of Tess. In Hardy's tragic vision the Fates were replaced by unconscious forces such as those of Darwinian sexual selection and heredity, which act through the fatal flaw in the character of the protagonist. Tess has a tendency to be both impulsive and dreamy: it is when she falls asleep, for example, that Prince is killed, putting in motion the entire train of tragic events; she leaps on Alec's horse on impulse and then promptly falls asleep; she accepts Angel's proposal in a state of reverie. For Hardy, therefore, the purity of Tess resides not simply in her struggle against external forces, but her efforts to master her internal desires. He emphasises this struggle through the development of a symbolic web within the novel, including such symbols as the D'Urberville coach (which appears whenever a 'crime' is committed) and the colour red, which project Tess towards her final crime. It is, therefore, not merely cosmetic that Hardy should greet her execution with the declaration that 'the President of the Immortals (in Aeschylean phrase) had ended his sport with Tess'.

> **Context**
>
> In the 1870s Hardy was reading imitations of Sophoclean tragedy such as Matthew Arnold's *Merope* (1858) and making notes for his own 'grand tragedy' or 'Iliad of Europe'. This project was later to take shape in *The Dynasts*, a modern verse drama about the Napoleonic wars in which Napoleon and Wellington are depicted as mere puppets in the hands of fate.

❮ Top ten *quotation*

Critical context

From serial to novel

Hardy, in common with authors such as Dickens, Eliot and Thackeray, first released his work through instalments in contemporary periodicals. This process had a significant impact on a novel's construction and

content: primarily, authors were subject to the censorship of editors sensitive to the fragile moral sensibilities of their readers; they also constructed their novels around easily identifiable 'cliff-hangers'; finally, they were able to respond to reader-response and adapt their stories accordingly (Hardy changed the ending of *The Return of the Native* because of public demand). In this context, the serialisation and novel publication of *Tess of the D'Urbervilles* provides an interesting account of the trials of authorship.

Hardy began writing the novel in the autumn of 1888 for publication in *Tillotson's Magazine*, but they were so horrified with the first half of the novel — which included sex in a wood, an illegitimate baby and an amateur baptism — that they refused to publish. Hardy's response was his essay 'Candour in English fiction' (1890), in which he argued that the dominance of the periodical press and the circulating library was harmful to serious contemporary fiction because they 'do not foster the growth of the novel that reflects and reveals life' but encouraged a saccharine version palatable for the whole family. Eventually, however, he gave in, removing the offending scenes (he even cynically wrote newly censored passages in a different coloured ink so that he knew what to change for novel publication) to ensure publication in *The Graphic*. Tess's seduction was now sanitised by a false marriage to Alec, and Angel carried the milkmaids across the ford in a wheelbarrow to avoid a compromising position. Immediately the run had finished, the novel appeared, in which he reinstated most of the bowdlerised scenes, though still omitting the racy Chaseborough dance (which is therefore not in the 2003 Penguin Classics edition). The novel format underwent several revisions, with a serious reduction of the use of dialect and a gradual harshening of the character of Angel, until the publication of the revised Wessex Edition of 1912, the version with which we are familiar.

Context of reception

The book was an immediate success with public and critics, the paperback edition selling 100,000 copies in 1900–01. Many of the latter judged it Hardy's masterpiece: *The Atlantic Monthly* asserted that it was 'Hardy's best novel yet' and *The Westminster* claimed that it was the greatest novel since the death of George Eliot. Even Henry James grudgingly acknowledged that, though it was 'chock-full of faults and falsities' it still possessed 'a singular beauty and charm'. There were, however, other voices raised in objection: *Harper's Weekly* noted that it was 'not in the reality of any sane world we recognise' while the

Saturday Review called the novel 'an unpleasant novel told in a very unpleasant way'.

Early criticism

Early Hardy criticism, like the early reviews of his books, tended to polarise opinion. G. K. Chesterton described him in *The Victorian Age in Literature* (1913) as 'a sort of village atheist brooding and blaspheming over the village idiot', while D. H. Lawrence in his *Study of Thomas Hardy* (1914) and E. M. Forster in *Aspects of the Novel* (1927) tended to accept Hardy as a great writer whose novels had been marred by his philosophising and moralising. The former, in particular, acknowledged Hardy as the main influence on his novels, particularly in his approach to sex and the unconscious. More objective criticism dates from the 1930s, when the humanist school of criticism, typified by the work of David Cecil, was in the ascendant. The focus of this school was on the ability of authors to create imaginative worlds that were a true reflection of the relationships of ordinary human beings to each other and their environment, a feat that Hardy, he argued in his *Hardy the Novelist* (1943), achieved. A reaction against this came with New Criticism, which abandoned biographical detail to focus on the words on the page and, for its British apologist, F. R. Leavis, the moral seriousness of the work. With New Criticism, Hardy became the subject of scrutiny in academic departments: as such it provides the starting point for a number of different critical schools.

Formalism and deconstruction

New Criticism, which embraced formalism, was the dominant critical tradition during the mid-twentieth century and invited readers to focus on the language, structure and patterns of imagery in a novel. The American critic Dorothy Van Ghent's *The English Novel: Form and Function* (1953) was important in asking the reader to give selected passages from Hardy (the garden scene being one) the same close reading as poetry and marvel at the construction. More recent critics, however, have supplemented close reading with the techniques of literary deconstruction advanced by the linguistic analysis of Ferdinand Saussure and Jacques Derrida. Deconstruction focuses on language and meaning, challenging the notion that texts consist of a single authoritative meaning since they are made up of words, and language is full of ambiguity. 'Meaning' therefore becomes slippery, the 'truth' of a

Pause for Thought

How far does the following critical view enhance your reading of the novel?

Hardy figures 'in literary criticism and literary history as a great novelist "in spite of" gross defects, the most commonly alleged of which are his manipulation of events in defiance of probability to produce a tragic-ironic pattern, his intrusiveness as authorial commentator, his reliance on stock characters, and his capacity for writing badly' (David Lodge, *The Language of Fiction,* 1966).

text relative to the interpretation of the words on the page by individual readers.

In the 1970s the American critic J. Hillis Miller employed such techniques to deconstruct Hardy's novels in his *Thomas Hardy: Distance and Desire* (1970). In his analysis of *Tess of the D'Urbervilles* he challenges the notion that the authorial interventions are Hardy's own voice guiding our moral responses, arguing instead that there is no single personality but a sequence of 'moments of vision, written as things seem first one way to him and then another'. There is no 'authorial intention' in the novel, no need to iron out philosophical inconsistencies because there is no overarching moral message in the novel: Tess suffers, but there is no reason in it. More recently, Deborah Collins, in *Thomas Hardy and his God* (1990), has arrived at the same conclusions, arguing that Hardy's constant disavowal of a single authorial voice freed him from 'danger of philosophical tunnel vision' and allowed him to explore the world around him through competing, and sometimes contradictory, voices.

Sociological criticism

Unlike formalist and deconstructive approaches, sociological criticism holds that both the production of literature and the way we read it are influenced by the cultural and political forces underpinning society. One particularly interesting approach is that of Peter Widdowson in his essay 'Hardy in history: a case study in the sociology of literature' (1983), which has sought to expose as a caricature the 'Hardy' constructed by criticism, the heritage industry and those who set A-level examinations. This Hardy is a nostalgic storyteller who introduces the reader to a lovingly evoked Wessex inhabited by a gallery of memorable characters participating in a number of closely observed pastoral rituals. His central theme of thwarted love is universal in its appeal and his prose is poetic with just enough theoretical underpinning to prevent the accusation of over-sentimentality.

A more ideologically rooted approach is offered by Marxist criticism, which emerged with Arnold Kettle's *Introduction to the English Novel* (1953) and has more recently informed the work of Terry Eagleton, particularly his *The English Novel from Dickens to Hardy* (1970). The Hardy who emerges from such an approach is a Victorian class-warrior trumpeting the rights of oppressed rural workers in both his novels and essays such as *The Dorsetshire Labourer* (1883). For Kettle, *Tess of the D'Urbervilles* is a novel of exploitation: Tess becomes a symbol of the rural proletariat exploited and destroyed by the new capitalist bourgeoisie symbolised by Alec, a theme played out largely by the

Pause for *Thought*

Widdowson notes of Polanski's film version of the text that it 'is remarkably faithful to the novel, but in its emphasis and focus, in its selections and inclusions, in its casting and filming, in its interpretative frame, it reproduces a reading that the novel will sustain, but which is essentially late twentieth century in its ideological orientation' (p. 124).

Do you agree with his view?

increasingly exploitative work practices and increasing mechanisation of bourgeois farmers such as Groby. The rural proletariat are alienated from the land that has been their livelihood, forced to sell their labour cheaply, and eventually forcefully dispossessed.

Psychoanalytical criticism

Hardy's writing career coincided with enormous developments in psychology, culminating in the psychoanalytical work of Sigmund Freud towards the end of the century. Hardy was fascinated by the 'unconscious', and he was continually seeking ways to represent its functioning in his novels. A number of critical studies, therefore, have found it fruitful to employ the conceptual framework and vocabulary of Freud to dissect Hardy's novels, Rosemary Sumner's *Thomas Hardy: Psychological Novelist* (1981) providing a good example. Freud sought to understand the power of the unconscious by splitting the mind into three: the id, which comprises unconscious instinctual impulses towards personal gratification (primarily sexual) and reveals itself in dreams; the superego, which is an internal censor bringing social pressures to bear upon the id; and the ego, which mediates between the sexual demands of the id and the demands of society through defensive processes such as repression. Such an interpretative framework has proved invaluable to critics analysing the creative processes and the degree to which writers exhibit and repress the neuroses of the societies in which they work. Did Hardy, for example, ever shake off the prejudices of the Victorian society he was so keen to criticise?

Using such an interpretative method, it is clear that the harshness of Tess's struggle emerges from the presence of a particularly strong id (a prematurely awakened sexuality combined with her hereditary disposition) and a highly refined, overly sensitive, superego. It is noticeable that, unlike Izz, who would have joined Angel in Brazil if it had not meant betraying a friend, Tess has internalised the moral strictures of a repressive society that condemns her sexual identity. Whereas Alec is all id, or 'animalism' as Hardy terms it, Angel's repressed sexuality is the result of a highly disciplined ego — what Hardy poetically describes as 'a hard logical deposit, like a vein of metal in a soft loam'. Hardy presents Angel's unconscious symbolically through his distortion of the Garden of Eden motif (according to which Tess becomes the snake), and episodes such as the sleepwalking, which reveals both the death of his love and where he puts the blame for Tess's behaviour — her hereditary disposition. Significantly, they appeal to different aspects of Tess, her relationship with Angel developing only after he has become more like Alec — whose 'animalism' is then no longer needed.

❮ Top ten *quotation*

Feminist criticism

By far the most popular interpretative tool employed in recent Hardy studies has been feminist criticism. In general it focuses on whether Hardy was able to produce convincing female characters and also the degree to which he was able to escape the misogyny of Victorian society in their creation. Thus, much work has sought to contextualise the novels within the sexual ideology of the period, Penny Boumelha's *Thomas Hardy and Women: Sexual Ideology and Narrative Form* (1982) providing an excellent example. Much has been made of the fact that, try as he might, Hardy's female characters remain the passive object of male gaze, especially his own. Tess, for example, is always under scrutiny in a way that the male characters in the novel are not, betraying Hardy's inherent misogyny. Furthermore, Tess remains a passive victim, waiting for a shift in male attitudes rather than asserting herself; embracing her fate as natural rather than the construct of an unfair patriarchy.

Other women in the novel are also represented unfavourably: Joan is a schemer willing to prostitute her daughter; Mercy Chant is a starched prig; Marian (jolly and plump) and Retty (descended from a once great family) come to terms with their loss of Angel through drink and attempted suicide; and the rest are either insensitive gossips or workers, such as Car Darch, brutalised and masculinised by their labour. Such unsympathetic characterisation provides ample evidence for those critics who claim that Hardy, despite his protestations, could never escape the misogynistic limitations imposed by the society in which he was writing.

More recent criticism, particularly that of Rosemarie Morgan's *Women and Sexuality in the Novels of Thomas Hardy* (1988) and the work of Nina Auerbach, has broadened the focus to include more generalised issues of gender and sexuality. Thus, Angel's repressed sexuality has re-emerged as a topic of interest in relation to the emergence of women who, for Morgan, are not victims but sexually active women willing to assert their sexuality in defiance of Victorian sensibilities. Auerbach concurs, arguing that Hardy uses the Garden of Eden motif in *Tess of the D'Urbervilles* to present a heroine whose sexual experience is a source of empowerment, allowing her to tower spiritually over the other characters in the novel, particularly her anaemic 'husband'. The Hardy who emerges from such studies is not a misogynist, but a writer attempting to explore the subject of female sexuality through metaphor and motifs in defiance of social attitudes uneasy with the notion of female desire.

Pause for *Thought*

Discuss the following feminist reading: 'For the feminist reader, clearly one of the most distressing features of *Tess of the D'Urbervilles* is the heroine's unrelieved humility... This extreme passivity can, as Mary Jacobus has shown, be partly explained by Hardy's anxiety about her purity. To absolve her from any responsibility for her downfall, he was forced to render her naïve and helpless, sometimes to the point of stupidity' (Lynne Pearce, 'Sexual Politics' in *Feminist Readings*, 1989).

Working with the text

Meeting the Assessment Objectives

AO1: Articulate creative, informed and relevant responses to literary texts, using appropriate terminology and concepts, and coherent, accurate written expression.

For AO1, you need to write fluently, structuring your essay carefully, guiding your reader clearly through your line of argument and using sophisticated vocabulary, including critical terminology, that is appropriate to an A-level essay. You will need to use frequent embedded quotations to give evidence of close detailed knowledge, and you should demonstrate familiarity with the whole text.

AO2: Demonstrate detailed critical understanding in analysing the ways in which structure, form and language shape meanings in literary texts.

In studying a text you should think about its overall structure (how it is organised, how its constituent parts connect with each other) and language. So, for *Tess of the D'Urbervilles* consider why Hardy has divided the novel into 'phases' and chapters headed by Roman numerals. In his other tragic novels he employs different conventions: in *Jude the Obscure* he divides the novel into 'Parts,' which introduce the different geographical locations in which the action unfolds; in *The Return of the Native* he uses the archaic 'Book the First' etc., the five-book structuring consciously resembling the five acts of a classical tragedy. The 'phases' of Tess suggest a chronological movement as Tess grows from youth to womanhood. In order to discuss language in detail you will need to quote from the text — but the mere act of quoting is not enough to meet AO2. What is important is what you do with the quotation — how you analyse it and how it illuminates your argument.

AO3 is a double assessment objective that asks you to 'explore connections and comparisons between different literary texts' as well as showing your understanding of the views and interpretations of others. It is important, therefore, to have some knowledge of other novels and poems by Hardy as well as work by contemporary writers whose work may have points of comparison and contrast with Tess. This critical guide has been prepared with this in mind and is full of references to other significant texts. However, it is not simply a matter of trotting out points of comparison. You must analyse what they show and how this information helps the development of your argument. When writing comparatively, use words and constructions that will help you to link your texts — such as, whereas, on the other hand, while, in contrast to, by comparison.

To access the second half of AO3, which asks you to 'look at various possible different interpretations and use these to develop your own' you need to remember that the text has no single 'meaning' but is open to interpretation. This works at sentence, symbolic and thematic level: you may want to give an alternative reading of a specific line (who is asking the question 'where was Tess's guardian angel?', the particular use of a symbol (the colour red seems to symbolise different qualities in different contexts and when seen through the eyes of different characters) or an entire theme (is Tess a powerful heroine in the tragic mode or a weak victim of male oppression?). Worthwhile AO3 means more than quoting someone else's point of view and saying you agree, although it can be very helpful to use critical views if they push forward an argument of your own. Look for other ways of reading texts — from a Marxist, feminist, new historicist, post-structuralist, psychoanalytic, dominant or oppositional point of view (all of which are alluded to in the *Contexts* section of this guide). Using modal verb phrases such as 'may be seen as', 'might be interpreted as' or 'could be represented as' implies that you are aware that different readers interpret texts in different ways at different times. The key word here is plurality. There is no single meaning, no right answer, and you need to evaluate a range of other ways of making textual meanings as you work towards your own.

AO4: Demonstrate understanding of the significance and influence of the contexts in which literary texts are written and received.

To access AO4 successfully you need to place the text at the heart of the web of contextual factors that you feel have had the most impact upon it. Examiners want to see a sense of contextual alertness woven seamlessly into the fabric of your essay rather than a clumsy bolted-on rehash of

…remember that the text has no single 'meaning' but is open to interpretation

a website or your old history notes. When studying a text like *Tess of the D'Urbervilles* it is often easy to forget that there is a gulf between its original contemporary context of production and the twenty-first-century context in which you 'receive' it. The *Contexts* section of this guide has suggested that Hardy's readers were preoccupied by subjects such as evolution, heredity, rural mobility and religion to a degree that we may find difficult to credit today. However, it is not enough to acknowledge, say, Hardy's interest Darwinian theory — you need to suggest how this interest may have influenced his characterisation of Tess. Furthermore, the novel is interesting in the way that it evolved in accordance with the gradual loosening of social constraints around it: the final novel version is very different from the heavily censored first serial version (see 'Critical context').

Essay questions and specimen plans

Coursework essays

General titles

1 In what ways is the novel an indictment of the late-Victorian class system?

2 Discuss the role of nature and fate in the novel.

3 Is Hardy a feminist writer?

4 Explore the character of Tess, showing how she develops through the novel, and compare your views with those of other commentators.

5 Compare Alec and Angel as both characters and men.

6 To what extent are the characters enriched by being woven into a rich tapestry of symbolism?

Creative (as in personal/original writing) interpretation

1 How does Hardy's way of structuring *Tess of the D'Urbervilles* affect your interpretation of the novel?

2 How does Hardy's use of imagery and symbolism affect your interpretation of the novel?

3 How does Hardy's use of different narrative voices affect your interpretation of the novel?

Creative/transformational writing

1 Write Tess's account of the moment when she reveals to Angel her past history. You should aim to write in Tess's voice, building upon Hardy's presentation of his character and capturing aspects of the writer's chosen form, structure and language.

2 Write Tess's thoughts as she sits alone in her dressing room, shortly before she kills Alec. You should aim to write in Tess's voice, building upon Hardy's presentation of his character and capturing aspects of the writer's chosen form, structure and language.

3 Write Angel's account of his first meeting with Tess. You should aim to write in Angel's voice, building upon Hardy's presentation of his character and capturing aspects of the writer's chosen form, structure and language.

Question 3: extract from sample answer

Oh the joys of nature and the simple country life. I had spent the morning walking through the Vale of Blakemore, a local derivation of the more traditional Blakemoor, listening to my brothers discoursing on the merits of *A Counterblast to Agnosticism,* when we came upon a local village festival. Its participants, all young girls dressed in white and waving the willow wand waved by Ariadne to the departing Odysseus, engaged in some Pagan festival that marked their progress to womanhood. 'Here,' I remarked to a scoffing Cuthbert, 'is more of a counterblast to agnosticism than is revealed by your theological texts. Here there is the vitality of our Hellenic forefathers!' I left him leaning on the fence, appalled at my heretical stance, whilst I went in search of a dance. One particular maiden had caught my eye, marked by a red ribbon and the most extraordinary beauty. Such a genuine daughter of Nature I had never seen; a new Eve. My path to her, however, was blocked by a more forthright maiden, who quickly had me dancing to a different tune from that I had intended.

The striking church clock brought me out of my reverie, reminded me of myself, my station and my duties. However, as I joined my brothers and ascended the hill I found myself pausing to regard the scene once more. There she stood, apart from her fellows, and I immediately regretted that I had not danced with her, thereby denying myself the pleasure and avoiding hurting her feelings. There was something in her modesty that set her apart from her more earthy companions. And those eyes, those lips...yes the lips that seemed so...godly, that they stayed with me for the rest of our journey home.

'And what do you take from your recent flirtation with the local peasantry,' sneered Cuthbert, 'and what would Mercy Chant say?' he added in a rather more pointed tone.

'I hope,' I replied, 'that she would recognise the spiritual value in such beauty,' and left it at that.

Student's own commentary

For my first-person narrative, I have emphasised the different spiritual perspective held by Angel and his brothers. Cuthbert I have presented as the dry academic suggested by the novel, his head buried in books and keen to remind Angel of his debt to Mercy Chant. I have drawn from my contextual knowledge to give Angel the tone of a naïve, Romantic enthusiast who is eager to find spiritual value in the simple pleasures of nature and the people who work in her, hence the Wordsworthian echoes of his opening statement. I have also drawn on Hardy's characterisation and emphasised Angel's pomposity through his pedantic reference to the derivation of Blakemore and his use of Classical analogies. I have employed Hardy's symbolism: the virginal white dresses; the willow wand signifying yearning love (a proleptic symbol for Tess); the red ribbon in her hair (marking her out like the hunted hart in the Vale). I have also emphasised Angel's attraction to the 'vitality' of this world (a common theme in the novel).

I have sought to present Angel's attraction to Tess within this 'pastoral' framework by incorporating the novel's reference to her as a 'genuine daughter of Nature' — an ironic description which plays upon the contrasting interpretation of nature as either idealised or brutally Darwinian. This irony is reinforced by his reference to Eve, through which he means to emphasise her purity, but by which he unwittingly identifies her as the author of his downfall. His failure to dance with Tess I have put down to a combination of his timidity, her natural modesty, and the intervention of fate in the form of the more forthright girl. I have incorporated the musical metaphor to emphasise that this intervention changes the entire 'composition' of his life. His attraction is made manifest through his reference to her 'eyes' and 'lips,' the latter repeated with ellipses to show that he cannot bring himself to admit to the possibility of an erotic attraction. He is called back to himself from his 'reverie', a term typical of Hardy since it emphasises the sleep of

❮ Top ten *quotation*

reason, by the church clock and the ecclesiastical world represented by his brothers. I have also made it quite clear that he is aware that in dancing with milkmaids he is acting beneath his social class.

Examiner's comments

AO1 — quality of writing:

- accurate spelling, punctuation and grammar
- vocabulary appropriate to a nineteenth-century gentleman
- a creative and original point of view (explaining Angel's attraction to Tess and why he failed to act on it)
- creating and sustaining a believable register
- no unnecessary narration or plot recount

AO2 — form, structure and language:

- the character chosen is understood and the attitudes he displays are convincing and likely, based upon a close reading of the text
- the language chosen is entirely appropriate for the character, with an acknowledgement that the opinions may be unreliable
- use of symbolism entirely in accordance with the novel
- specific references to Hardy's text, which shows a seamless overarching understanding of the text

AO3 — different interpretations:

- offers a fresh understanding of Angel's thoughts at a pivotal moment of the text, without narrative comment

AO4 — contexts:

- actions and speech appropriate to the era in which the text is set
- references to the Romantic movement, nineteenth-century church debates, and Hellenism

Exam essays

Passage-based essay questions

Here are the questions to address when analysing a passage from *Tess of the D'Urbervilles*:

- Why has Hardy included this passage in the novel? What is its importance?
- How does this passage fit into the narrative structure of the novel?

- Which of the themes is Hardy evoking here, and how does this passage fit into his treatment of that theme in the whole novel?

- What previous scenes do we need to recall in order to understand fully the implications of this passage?

- Does this extract foreshadow any future scenes?

- What is the narrative voice and does it shift to give the subjective experience of any single character? Is Hardy himself present in the narration?

- Does Hardy use any recurring images or symbols in this passage? If so, analyse how they fit into the overall pattern.

- If there is some description, what mood is Hardy evoking and how does he do it?

- Is there any speech in this passage? If so, what does it add to the effectiveness, and what does it tell us about the speaker?

- Are there any particular words or metaphors that would reward close analysis?

- Is this one of the times when Hardy uses the present tense to give a sense of immediacy and involve the reader?

Passage-based question with prompts

Look again at Chapter IX. Then answer the following questions:
(i) What do you learn about Alec's character in this chapter?
(ii) How does Hardy tell the story in this chapter?
(iii) Some readers think that Alec D'Urbervilles is simply a stereotypical villain. What do you think about his character and role in the whole novel?

The following is an examiner's report based on this question:
(i) Mocking, egotistical, manipulative, sexual predator, taunting, assertive, disrespectful of mother, sinister, dominating, self conscious, cruel etc.

(ii) Structure — gentle, quiet opening describing Tess in a natural setting as supervisor of poultry, dramatic centre of Alec forcibly teaching Tess to whistle, sinister end where Hardy tells us that Alec secretly spies on Tess, simple and Latinate language, omniscient narration, use of detail, use of dialogue, motif of the birds, religious imagery, allusions to Shakespeare, use of time etc.

(iii) Some will agree, reference might be made to his appearance, his behaviour, his seduction and rape of Tess, his pursuit of her, his deceit and lying, his link with the devil, his farcical conversion. Some will disagree and see his conversion as sincere or a genuine attempt to confront his sinful past. Some will see his behaviour as

psychologically convincing in terms of an obsessive temperament; some will see him as being psychologically convincing and as being spoilt and without moral guidance. Some will see him as a representative of the new middle class, as a representative of a rake. Some might focus on the fact that he does not abandon Tess and that she does stay with him for a while. Some might say that there is something attractive about him. Some will see him as directly responsible for Tess's death. Some might see him as adding to the theme of ancestry (at the end when he appears at the D'Urberville vault he is commanding — like a medieval nobleman, perhaps). Some will compare him with Clare etc.

Passage-based question without prompts

Read the opening of Phase the Fifth running from 'Her narrative ended…the woman I have been loving is not you.'

Comment on and analyse how the writer's choices of structure, form and language shape meaning.

In an answer you should be focusing on the following:

- Hardy dismisses the climactic delivery with his arresting opening statement: he is more interested in the consequence.

- Hardy sets her account against an uncaring universe: the account that has such an impact on Tess has no effect on the material objects, indeed, Hardy's universal process, personified in the shape of the fire, seems to laugh 'as if it did not care in the least about her strait'. Later in the chapter Hardy reinforces this idea with his observation that 'Time was chanting his satiric psalm at her'.

- Hardy switches his interest to the power of words — the endearments seeming to be expressions of 'purblind foolishness' (echoing their previous representation as 'simpletons'), which are personified and 'hustle away' to be replaced by her 'narrative'.

- Focus switches to Angel: his reaction is first recorded physiologically, his withering face anticipating the harsh effects of Brazil. Stirring of fire is a meaningless act.

- The dialogue that follows is deliberately stilted, words are not equal to the occasion, 'the perfunctory babble of the surface'. The ellipsis in Angel's speech suggests his state of shock while his repetition of the personal pronoun and in particular the possessive 'My wife, my Tess' emphasises his egotism.

- Tess also abases herself on her knees in front of him, but her reasoning, though delivered in a state of shocked panic and becoming increasingly desperate and incredulous, is perfectly sound:

'Forgive me as you are forgiven! I forgive you, Angel.'

'You — yes, you do.'

'But you do not forgive me?'

The repetition of the pronouns 'you', 'me', 'I' highlights the problem of altered identity that lies at the centre of this passage.

- Tess maintains her belief in Angel despite his confession but, as he candidly makes clear, Tess's confession changes her very identity for him: 'I repeat, the woman I have been loving is not you.' There is an intense irony here because he has just physically transformed her into a D'Urberville.

- Also important is the way that Angel slips back into religious language in his condemnation of 'such a grotesque — prestidigitation as that!'

- His demonic laugh picks up on that of the fire and also that of Alec in his most Satanic guise.

Passage-based questions with comparative texts

1 'Tess is very responsive to the atmosphere of the places where she lives.'

Using *Tess of the D'Urbervilles* from the beginning of Chapter III 'The interior, in spite of the melody...' to '"Where is father now?" asked Tess suddenly', explore the presentation of the reaction of Tess to her surroundings.

In your response, you should focus on *Tess of the D'Urbervilles* to establish your argument and you should refer to the second text you have read to support and develop your line of argument.

2 'Tess is very responsive to nature and its moods.'

Using *Tess of the D'Urbervilles* Chapter XVI as your starting point, from 'Either the change in the quality of the air' to 'when the dairymen set about getting in the cows', explore the presentation of natural surroundings and the effect on Tess.

In your response, you should focus on *Tess of the D'Urbervilles* to establish your argument and you should refer to the second text you have read to support and develop your line of argument.

Whole-text essay questions

Response to a proposition

1 'Melodramatic rather than tragic.' How apt a description of the novel do you find this?

2 Consider the judgement of *Tess of the D'Urbervilles* as 'full of faults, but a very great novel'.

3 'A pure woman.' How far do you agree that Hardy was justified in describing Tess in this way?

4 'Despite the element of sheer bad luck, *Tess of the D'Urbervilles* has a tragic inevitability.' Do you agree?

Whole-text comparative

1 What use do authors in the pastoral tradition make of oppositions between the urban and the rural?

2 To what extent is a pastoral treatment of the past inevitably prettified and nostalgic?

3 'The concept of the rural ideal is a complex one, involving many different attitudes and values.' Discuss this view.

Comparison with named text

1 'Writers present us with a clear sense of values. These values are drawn into particularly sharp focus when a chief concern of their writing is emotion.'

Comment on and analyse the connections and comparisons between *Tess of the D'Urbervilles* and *Captain Corelli's Mandolin* in the light of this assertion.

In your response you should demonstrate what it means to be considering texts as a modern reader, in a modern context and that other readers at other times may well have had other responses.

2 'Literature provides us with countless examples that prove the fact that men have difficulty imagining female lives.'

Comment on and analyse the connections and comparisons between at least two texts you have studied in the light of this comment.

3 'We have only the word "love", yet we understand it to mean so much. There are so many different kinds of love that one single word cannot possibly do for them all.'

Comment on and analyse the connections and comparisons between *Tess of the D'Urbevilles* and *Captain Corelli's Mandolin* in the light of this comment.

Question 3: suggested plan

For this question you need to focus on different types of love: romantic love, familial love, love of duty, material love, love of God, comradely love and patriotic love.

To some extent the central message of both novels is that love is a product of sacrifice. The most important type of love addressed by both novels is romantic love, and so this should take up a large part of your essay. When dealing with this issue you should include some of the following points:

- Both Tess and Pelagia are trapped in love triangles, stranded in a state of powerlessness between the attentions of two men.
- The tendency of men to idealise women is a quality shared by both Angel and Mandras. The beauty of both Tess and Pelagia makes them victims of male sexual advances. Their fate is to be contrasted with that of the plain Retty and Drosoula.
- The importance of chastity in both Mediterranean culture and that of nineteenth-century England.
- The importance of music as a means of expressing emotions in both novels: Alec seduces Tess by teaching her to whistle and she is subsequently attracted by Angel's harp. Similarly, it is through music that Corelli captures Pelagia's heart.
- Both women are victims of sexual violence: Alec's seduction/rape, and Mandras's attempted rape.
- Both Tess and Pelagia are also victims of forces beyond their control, which throw them into the arms of men. Tess is ground down by her poverty and Hardy's series of coincidences. Pelagia is forced to endure war, the communist takeover and the death of her father.

You will also need to cover:

- Familial love: this should include Tess's love of her parents, despite having little cause, and also her love of her siblings — particularly 'Liza-Lu. Pelagia loves her father, helping him with his medical practice and his writing of his 'History', and also Drosoula, a surrogate mother.
- Comradely love and how this is transformed into Carlo's homosexual love for Corelli; his sacrifice presents a different kind of pure love.
- Love of humanity, as displayed by Dr Iannis, Corelli and Old Mr Clare and Angel.
- Love of doctrine: Mandras's misguided love for his new communist vision; Weber for his Nazism; and Angel for his inhumane humanism. Within this you can also discuss patriotic love as shown by Mandras, Kokolios and Stamatis.
- Love of God, through the conflicting views of Arsenios, the itinerant sign-painter, Tess, Alec and Angel.

Sample essay, passage-based

Read the garden scene in Chapter XIX from 'it was a typical summer evening in June' to 'drive all such horrid fancies away!'
Comment on and analyse how the writer's choices of structure, form and language shape meaning.

This scene is important in the novel because it reveals the sexual passion that Tess has for the young Angel Clare, through the medium of music. Accordingly, it transforms her desire into one more thing that she must fight against in order to maintain her integrity.

The setting is, in typical Hardy fashion, both general and specific, an echo of the opening line of the novel, which has the effect of raising this encounter to the level of the universal. The atmosphere is magical: a 'delicate equilibrium' with even inanimate objects endowed with senses and the silence a 'positive entity' rather than a negation. The silence is disturbed by Angel's poorly played second-hand harp. Once again the intruder in a rural scene, his poor execution warns us that he is no Angel. Indeed, if he is to play the part of any biblical character in this scene then he is more an Adam playing opposite to Tess's Eve, a relationship that Hardy invokes repeatedly to characterise their courtship. If, however, they are the first two people on the earth, then Tess through her 'crime' has already been expelled from the sanitised Eden of the creationist myth to an uncultivated portion of the garden where 'the rank-smelling weed-flower glowed'. Here Hardy evokes nature governed by Darwinian rules of sexual selection to describe a garden teeming with sensuous sexuality. As Angel's notes penetrate the silence, they are transformed through a process of synaesthesia into a metaphor for sexual attraction: they have a 'stark quality like that of nudity' and mix with the pollen (the most visible reproductive element of nature).

Some critics have chosen to focus on the moral aspects of the scene, arguing that, while the harp is attracting Tess's sexual nature, her purity is maintained because her spirit has been removed in a way similar to the effects of 'gazing at a star'. But this is not how the passage reads. For Hardy, the fallen Tess is simply an extension of the natural laws surrounding her; accordingly, Angel's harmonies are not simply heard, but 'passed like breezes through her', evoking the same intensely sensual reaction that marks Hardy's description of the garden. She is transformed into a 'fascinated bird' and then a 'cat', led without a will of her own. The sound of the notes is supplemented by the onomatopoeia of the 'cracking snails'

ur...
m...
t...
t...
s...
l...

tree:
on th..ety
that finds the sexual in nature beautiful but condemns it when manifested
in any woman. Tess remains stained by the man who is the blood-red ray in
her life — Alec D'Urberville.

It is noticeable that Angel remains in the cultivated portion of the garden,
allowing him to continue to idealise nature. Whereas he moves in a
'desultorily' and 'rambling' way, and is unaware of the passion he has
unleashed, she is flushed and 'furtive', immediately establishing the dynamic
of their relationship as one of casual negligence and passionate secrecy.
His questioning is reported in mimetic form, Hardy withdrawing his narrative
voice to leave free direct speech without reporting clauses. The effect
is that it sounds more like an interrogation than courtship, Hardy clearly
emphasising Angel's 'hard logical deposit' at the expense of his humanity. ❰ Top ten *quotation*
It is music that brings them together; language is always awkward between
them. Angel addresses her as a simple milkmaid, patronising her, as he
does throughout the novel, by suggesting that her melancholy must stem
from her fear of the 'milk turning sour'. Through her response, however,
which begins with the platitude, 'life in general', Hardy transforms the whole
tone of the passage, leading to a clear statement of Tess's pessimism.

Through suitably pastoral imagery Tess lights upon what Hardy later terms
'the ache of modernism', her fear that she is trapped in a historical cycle ❰ Top ten *quotation*
set out by her hereditary ancestors. Through his use of personified rivers
and trees and the transformation of the future into 'to-morrows just all
in a line', Hardy attempts to convince the reader that such pessimism is
natural to Tess. Her fear is made dramatic through the choice of emotive
words such as 'fierce' and 'cruel', and the repetition of 'beware', combined
with the exclamation marks and ellipsis, suggests that Tess breaks off in a
state of some emotional excitement. Angel's reaction is unrecorded beyond
his surprise that a mere milkmaid could be responsible for 'shaping such
sad imaginings'. He is clearly out of his depth in emotional terms, a fact
that Tess stumbles on in her comments about his music. It is quite true that

for Angel music is a diversion from the world — much like his continual idealisation of it — whereas it places her directly in a world of yearning and desire.

This essay would have earned an A grade. For further sample essays with A and C answers and examiner's comments go to **www.philipallan. co.uk/literatureguidesonline**

Top ten quotations

1

Why it was that upon this beautiful feminine tissue, sensitive as gossamer, and practically blank as snow as yet, there should have been traced such a coarse pattern as it was doomed to receive; why so often the coarse appropriates the finer thus, many thousand years of analytical philosophy have failed to explain to our sense of order. (p. 74)

Hardy sets out the harsh paradox central to this story and, indeed, all his fiction: why do the most sensitive feminine qualities attract the coarsest masculine attributes. In the 1895 edition he added the aphoristic — 'the wrong man the woman, the wrong woman the man' — making explicit our tendency to end up with the wrong partners. Women are presented as delicate (like 'gossamer'), and pure as snow, 'doomed' (a term that suggests a fatalism) to be moulded by the desires of men. The 'coarse pattern', however, has a secondary meaning: it refers not only to external male desire, but also those internal desires shaped by evolutionary forces beyond individual control, such as the forces of hereditary disposition and Darwinian sexual selection.

2

'What a genuine daughter of Nature that milkmaid is!' he said to himself. (p. 120)

Angel lives in a 'pastoral' dream (see 'Pastoralism' in the *Contexts* section (pp. 67–68 of this guide)) in which he equates closeness to nature, here capitalised to give a sense of a personified mother Nature, with purity. Interestingly, in later editions of the novel he replaced 'genuine' with 'fresh and virginal', thereby making explicit that he (in common with Victorian society as a whole) equates purity with virginity. Significantly, when he learns of her history, he claims: 'Here was I thinking you a new-sprung child of nature; there were you, the exhausted seedling of an effete aristocracy' (p. 232)

> She was expressing in her own native phrases — assisted a
> little by her Sixth Standard training — feelings which might
> almost have been called those of the age — the ache of
> modernism. (p. 124)

3

This authorial interjection refers to Tess' pessimism, articulated through
the image of life as a parade of fierce and cruel tomorrows that
announce that 'I am coming! Beware of me!' (see Pessimism context).
Tess is caught between two worlds: the old rural world of her parents
(with its strong sense of community and harsh fatalism), and the new
world with its advanced technology, new bourgeois social structures, and
dogmatic ethical codes. Unfortunately, Tess has been educated out of the
first (with which Hardy remains broadly sympathetic) and has yet to join
the second. She finds herself continually displaced, which is why she is
so often depicted journeying from one location to the next.

> She was yawning, and he saw the red interior of her mouth
> as if it had been a snake's. She had stretched one arm so
> high above her coiled-up cable of hair that he could see
> its satin delicacy...It was a moment when a woman's soul
> is more incarnate than at any other time; when the most
> spiritual beauty bespeaks itself flesh... (p. 169)

4

Here we see Tess through Angel's loving eyes: she is sleepy and
vulnerable, the very essence of womanhood that he is prepared to
devote himself to protecting. He has continually regarded her as his Eve
(see Sexual hypocrisy: the 'fallen woman' theme), and distanced himself
from his erotic attraction, which is encoded in her presentation as the
serpent. The reference to 'woman's soul' is ambiguous because we are
unsure whether such reflections are attributable to Angel or Hardy. If the
latter, it offers ammunition for those who claim that Hardy was unable to
shake off the misogyny of Victorian society.

> her fine features were unquestionably traceable in these
> exaggerated forms. (p. 217)

5

When looking at the paintings of the D'Urberville women, Angel is
thinking about Tess. It is important to understand that Tess's actions
are, to some extent, guided by her barbaric hereditary ancestry (indeed,
Hardy changed the novel's title from *Too Late, Beloved* to emphasise
this fact). In this scene, Hardy makes Tess's powerlessness quite clear,
emphasising it further through Angel's closer inspection, which reveals
that a 'sinister design lurked in the woman's features, a concentrated
purpose of revenge on the other sex — so it seemed to him then' (pp.
234–5). This acts as a proleptic marker for his later condemnation of
Tess.

6 Within the remote depths of his constitution, so gentle and affectionate as he was in general, there lay hidden a hard logical deposit, like a vein of metal in a soft loam, which turned the edge of everything that attempted to traverse it. It had blocked his way with the Church; it blocked his way with Tess. (p. 241)

It is important to understand the psychology of Angel, because his rejection of Tess is so sudden and final. Hardy offers a suitably agricultural metaphor to illustrate his obstinacy; he appears soft, but his principles, built upon logic rather than emotion, are like metal. His rejection of Tess is placed within the context of his refusal to join the church. He sought to 'believe' in Tess but, when she falls short of his idealised projection, he rejects her out of disappointment and on a matter of principle.

7 'Now, punish me!' she said, turning up her eyes to him with the hopeless defiance of the sparrow's gaze before its captor twists its neck. 'Whip me, crush me...Once victim, always victim — that's the law!' (p. 332)

Tess, has bloodied Alec's face with her work gauntlet. The role of Tess as victim has been represented throughout the novel through bird imagery (see 'Birds' in the *Form, structure and language* section (pp. 51–52 of this guide)) and the scene when she beds down with the dying pheasants (pp. 278–79). Here her victimisation is entwined with the D'Urberville ancestry: her leather gauntlet is a debased form of that worn by her distant ancestors; the blood drawn reminds us that Alec is the 'blood red ray in the spectrum of her young life' (p. 42). It is a moment of defiance mixed with fatalistic submission, in which Tess acknowledges the law of nature made clear by Hardy's rhetorical questions at the beginning of the novel: the innocent and weak will always be crushed by the strong.

8 Who was the moral man? Still more pertinently, who was the moral woman? The beauty or ugliness of a character lay not only in its achievements, but in its aims and impulses... (p. 340)

His time in the harsh climate of Brazil causes Angel to question his belief in humanist moral codes in the same way that he had questioned church teachings. The deathbed advice of a friend that 'what Tess had been was of no importance beside what she would be...' (p. 341) leads him to conclude that in morality intention is more important than consequence.

9 'A jester might say this is just like Paradise. You are Eve, and I am the old Other One come to tempt you in the disguise of an inferior animal.' (pp. 348–49)

Initially this appears to clarify the binary relationship that juxtaposes Alec with Angel (Hardy even gives him a fork to contrast with Angel's harp). However, Alec's self-knowledge is offered as a refreshing contrast to Angel's delusion. In acknowledging his failings, he becomes human in a way that Angel's strong idealistic strain never allows; his failings are simply those you would expect in a world devised by a 'joker'.

| **'Justice' was done, and the President of the Immortals (in Aeschylean phrase) had ended his sport with Tess. (p. 397)** | **10** |

Throughout the novel, Tess is the victim of forces, both external (economic, social, religious) and internal (heredity, sexual), against which she is forced to struggle in order to maintain her sense of 'purity'. The fact that a patriarchal society condemns Tess rather than the predatory behaviour of men like Alec, combined with a church that refuses Sorrow a baptism while embracing Alec to its bosom, gives rise to Hardy's ironic use of the word 'justice'. Although Hardy was to distance himself from the sentiments contained in the quotation, arguing that it is a direct quotation from Aeschylus's *Prometheus*, such views echo his belief in the 'mockery' of human existence.

Taking it further

Criticism

- Eagleton, T. (2004) *The English Novel: An Introduction*, Blackwell.
  - A text that clearly and stylishly contextualises the novel within Hardy's other writings and the prevailing literary movements of the nineteenth century.
- Ebbatson, R. (1982) *The Evolutionary Self: Hardy, Forster, Lawrence*, Harvester.
  - A clear account of the relationship between evolutionary theory and Hardy's writing.
- Gatrell, S. (1993) *Thomas Hardy and the Proper Study of Mankind*, Macmillan.
- Gregor, I. (1974) *The Great Web: The Form of Hardy's Major Fiction*, Faber and Faber.
  - In a very clear style, Gregor explores some of the common themes that unite Hardy's novels.

- Kramer, D. (ed.) (1975) *Critical Essays on Thomas Hardy*, Macmillan.
  – A series of accessible academic essays focusing on the 'tragic' novels.
- Kramer, D. (ed.) (1999) *The Cambridge Companion to Thomas Hardy*, Cambridge University Press.
  – Soon to be superseded by the latest Cambridge Companion, but still excellent, bringing together preeminent Hardy scholars.
- Miller, J. H. (1970) *Thomas Hardy: Distance and Desire*, Harvard University Press.
  – Revolutionary in its day, this critical study still provides some of the most thought-provoking readings of Hardy's novels.
- Millgate, M. (1994) *Thomas Hardy: His Career as a Novelist*, Macmillan.
  – Comprehensive and elegantly constructed biography.
- Morgan, R. (1988) *Women and Sexuality in the Novels of Thomas Hardy*, Routledge.
  – An excellent feminist exploration of Hardy's female characters.
- Morgan, R. (2010) *Companion to Thomas Hardy*, Ashgate.
  – Bringing together Hardy scholars from all over the world, this offers scope for some more advanced research into his work.

Films and television

- **1980:** Directed by Roman Polanski with Nastassja Kinski and Peter Firth.
- **1998:** Directed by Ian Sharp with Justine Waddell and Jason Flemyng.
- **2008:** BBC drama production with Gemma Arterton

Websites

- The Thomas Hardy Society: **www.hardysociety.org**
- The Victorian Web is a resource for all nineteenth-century literature: **www.victorianweb.org**; click on 'Authors' to access Hardy specifically
- Quotations from other Hardy texts: **www.literary-quotations.com** (click on 'More authors')
- A gallery of the illustrations used in the Graphic edition of the novel: **www.victorianweb.org/art/** (click on 'Victorian Illustration', then 'Titles of Victorian Illustrated Books', then 'Tess of the D'Urbervilles'
- A 'concordance' of the novel is available at: **www.doc.ic.ac. uk/~rac101/concord/texts/tess/**, or search the internet for 'Tess of the D'Urbervilles concordance'